CW00919749

SCOTNOTES 2

THE POETRY OF EDWIN MORGAN

SECOND EDITION

This volume replaces the excellent previous edition, written
by the late Geddes Thomson, which covered Edwin Morgan's
work to 1986. The ASLS wishes to pay tribute to
Mr Thomson's volume as a model of clarity and precision,
which has been of invaluable assistance to students
of all ages wishing to become familiar with the poetry of
Edwin Morgan.

SCOTNOTES
Number 2

The Poetry of
Edwin Morgan

SECOND EDITION

James McGonigal

Association for Scottish Literary Studies 2013

Published by
Association for Scottish Literary Studies
Scottish Literature
7 University Gardens
University of Glasgow
Glasgow G12 8QH
www.asls.org.uk

ASLS is a registered charity no. SC006535

First edition published 1986 – written by Geddes Thomson

Second edition published 2013

A CIP catalogue for this title
is available from the British Library

ISBN 978-1-906841-15-7

The Association for Scottish Literary Studies
acknowledges the support of Creative Scotland
towards the publication of this book.

Printed by Bell and Bain Ltd, Glasgow

CONTENTS

CONTENTS (CONTINUED)

Page

ACKNOWLEDGEMENTS

I would like to thank the Education Committee of the Association for Scottish Literary Studies for entrusting me with this work. I appreciated the helpful editorial guidance of Ronnie Renton and Lorna Smith. Michael Schmidt of Carcanet Press and Hamish Whyte of Mariscat Press kindly allowed me to quote from poetry collections which they first published, and the Edwin Morgan Trust (SCIO) which now looks after the poet's literary affairs also gave its permission. The research support provided by staff in the Department of Special Collections in the University of Glasgow Library, where the Edwin Morgan Papers are lodged, has been exemplary.

A NOTE ON THE POEMS USED

Edwin Morgan's *New Selected Poems* (Carcanet Press, 2000) is used throughout, and most page references refer to this accessible collection. Where other poems are referred to, the full title of the relevant volume is given. Publication details and additional print and electronic resources are provided in Further Reading, and there is an Index of Titles of poems discussed.

1. INTRODUCTION

An inter/national poet

Edwin Morgan (1920–2010) is a poet whose work is very clear yet also quite complex. The clarity comes from the way he focuses on life, even when the poetry seems just witty or playful. He constantly reworks old forms and invents new ones as he responds to a modern world that changed radically in his lifetime. He wants his readers to look at this world almost as scientists: to examine what is happening around us, to weigh up the range of human behaviour, to listen in our imaginations to different voices and viewpoints – and to learn from all of this evidence what it means to be human. So there is great range to his poetry, and this is what makes it interesting but also complex to grasp as a whole. Under the title *The Poetry of Edwin Morgan* can we exclude his poetic translations, his verse drama and even his own critical writing on poetry?

It might be simpler, then, to focus on him as a Scottish poet, as the first National Poet. That is helpful, but only if we remember that, despite of his great love of Scotland, he was never content to live within narrow borders. He wanted the Scots to raise their sights beyond familiar ideas, to look outwards with confidence to other possibilities, and indeed to other worlds in time and space. His ceaseless work of translation from more than a dozen languages was one aspect of that outward-looking spirit. He was given the title 'The Scots Makar' by the Labour Executive in Scotland in 2004, shortly before the opening of the Scottish Parliament's ultra-modern building on Edinburgh's Royal Mile. Although happy to take on this national role, he had some doubts about that use of the medieval Scots word for poet (a makar is simply 'a maker' of poems), because it seemed backward-looking. Even at the age of eighty-four he favoured going forward, and saw the poet laureate's role as being to provide a guiding voice on that journey. And often when his poetry does reflect on images from the past, as in his *Sonnets from Scotland* (1984), it does so as part of a time-travelling journey that reveals new and surprising evidence of life in the land we now call Scotland, in the past as well as in its imagined futures.

It is not easy, then, to sum up the work of such a free-wheeling, varied and responsive poetic imagination. It might be helpful to rely on the poet's own choice in his *New Selected Poems* published in 2000, when he was eighty. These are the poems that he thought really caught what he was about – the ones he liked best and that audiences at poetry readings responded to as well. He was an excellent and frequent performer of his own work, and judging audience reaction was part of that. But there were also four main collections and two books of translation published after 2000, in the last decade of his life. Those can't be forgotten.

Key themes
In that wide-ranging work, key themes can be signposts. One of these is Glasgow, the city where he was born and lived for most of his long life. But this real city is also 'Everycity'. In some moods it has a pulse like New York, a place of restless energy and constant rebuilding. In others it is a post-industrial site of violence, unemployment and lost dignity, redeemed only by its ironic humour and refusal to be put down. Yet again it is Clydegrad, shining in some spectacular and fairer social-ist future where 'mile-high buildings flashed […]'. Glasgow is a mysteriously shifting place, a chameleon city where many lessons can be learned, if we keep our eyes and minds open. One thing that Morgan learned in a great industrial city was not to distrust or despise machines, as some earlier poets had done. Instead he admired technology as a witness to human craft and ingenuity. Urban life in all its variety is where most people must make their way, and the poet shares that life.

Politics is another theme in Morgan's work, considered as a broad spectrum. It includes those beliefs and decisions which create national and personal identity, which shape regional economies and share out resources. Politics expresses, in the end, what is thought worth fighting for. His life-experience included the 1930s Depression, service in the Royal Army Medical Corps in the Second World War, then the Cold War and atomic arms race between the great communist and capi-talist powers that followed from that war, and the adjustment of social values and sexual politics in the 1960s. With his fellow

Scots he lived through a series of political and economic crises in the last decades of the twentieth century. Thus we find him engaging in his writing with both Christianity and Communism as shapers of people's beliefs, using poetry to question the way things are.

Love is another central theme. His love poetry is often direct and affecting, creating a sense of vulnerability and tenderness. As a gay person at a time when homosexual activity was illegal (the law was liberalised in England in 1967, but not until 1980 in Scotland), he learned to write love poems where gender was not explicit, or where the language was coded to some extent. As a result, his view that human love was love, regardless of sexualities, became accepted by readers who had always responded to those poems in terms of their own experience of close relationships. Again, the range of emotions expressed is complex. Most memorable are the poems of intimate and fleeting moments, recognisable to anyone who has ever fallen in love. Yet physicality, transgression and loss are there too, as part of the story.

That last word reminds us that Morgan often described himself as a storyteller. Narrative is therefore another key feature of his work. There are different ways of telling stories, of course. Sometimes it is a life story, as in his poem 'Cinquevalli' on the career and death of an amazing acrobat and juggler. Often he creates fictions in a cinematic way, the story being told through juxtaposed images and multiple viewpoints (as in his 'Stobhill' sequence about an abortion). All human beings change with the passing of time, but in his narrative science-fiction poetry the time-travelling voyagers can find their attitudes changed forever by encounters with earlier human beings, as in 'From the Domain of Arnheim' and 'In Sobieski's Shield'. The late sequence 'Planet Wave', composed for jazz accompaniment, is itself the story of time, from the origins of the universe through life on earth and on to the edges of space, in explorations yet to come.

Language is central to his work, or rather a whole range of languages and codes. Morgan was a poet of many voices. To be a lyric poet with a clearly identifiable voice on the page, such as Norman MacCaig or Seamus Heaney, was not what

he wanted. Instead the reader is presented with multiple
'selves': a computer speaks, or an apple, a Loch Ness Monster,
a centaur, a Mercurian, St Columba, Shakespeare, Jesus
Christ, a drunk man on a bus, and many more. His translations were also a way of trying out fresh voices and personalities
– Russian, Hungarian, Italian, German, Old English, French
and Scots. His verse dramas of the 1990s extend that practice.
Morgan's translation of *Phèdre*, the French classical tragedy
by Jean Racine (1639–1699), has the characters speaking in
Scots.

Language itself is to be explored to its farthest boundaries
of verbal sound and written signs. Morgan's 'sound poetry'
plays with rhythm, pitch, letter and word patterns and the
emergence or decay of understanding. This experimentation
with sound was one strand of international avant-garde poetry
from the 1960s onwards in Britain. But Morgan had encountered it even earlier in Russian Futurist literature, with the
brief flourishing of experimental Zaum poetry of sheer noise
in the decade of the First World War, and also in European
literature, after the trauma of that war, with the nihilistic
poetry of the Dadaist poets in Switzerland, Germany and
France. His international outlook and adeptness in European
and Slavonic languages gave him entry to such poetry, which
also presented a challenge to any narrow definitions of what
Scottish poetry should be. So 'The Loch Ness Monster's Song'
is not merely a local poem, but part of a wider experimental
movement exploring sound and meaning.

Such artistic movements were connected with modern paint-
ing too, and 'concrete poetry' (developing from the late 1950s
onwards in Brazil and Switzerland) worked at the opposite
extreme from sound, namely at the visual pictorial edge of
words and letters as signs and patterns that appear on a page
– or on a poster, a wall or a sculpture. The concrete poets
wanted to cut language free of false rhetoric or self-expression,
and return it to the eye and mind in a pure form. Their aim
was to provoke thoughtfulness and a close regard for the way
words move and meanings take shape. There were various
kinds of concrete poetry, but Morgan's is notable not only for
its wit but also for the way he uses it to explore politics, as in

'Sharpeville', based on a racist massacre in South Africa, or religion, as in 'Message Clear'.

It is worth noting that he was criticised by more mainstream Scottish poets in the 1960s for his 'concrete-mixing', which they considered trivial. His own point of view was that ignoring or opposing such vibrant international movements would be fatal to the health of Scottish poetry. All kinds of poetry could be written, and should be. He resented that sort of narrow prescriptive or conservative approach which he felt had a detrimental impact on Scottish society in general. He allied himself with younger and more experimental poets in this regard. Yet at this very same point in time he was beginning to write those accessible poems about Glasgow, its street-life and its people, which opened up his poetry to new and younger readers.

The Scots Makar

From that brief outline, it is probably clear why he was the obvious candidate for the role of Scottish Makar or National Poet. No other poet could match him in range of work or in ability to connect with readers of all ages. But what did he think was the Makar's work? In 2009 he was asked by the Royal Society of Literature to comment on the role of the UK's Poet Laureate. Did the Laureateship have any useful place in modern society? With some reservations about the old-fashioned title, he thought that it did indeed have a purpose:

> We do require some person who can provide a kind of clarion call to the country, or a warning voice for a change of direction, if that is necessary. [...] The Laureateship needs a commanding presence, then, and certainly not someone tied to any narrow party version of truth.

Then very typically he looks outwards, to describe one poem in particular by a young nineteenth-century Hungarian poet, Sandór Petőfi, whose 'Nemzeti Dal' or 'National Song' had an immediate popular impact on his country as it struggled to throw off Austrian and Russian rule. The point was that poetry, at this national or laureate level, 'should remind people that

if they want to achieve something in the world, and to really
be taken seriously, then they need to show the world what
they stand for. And surely those who are best equipped to
articulate this are good writers, and this includes poets'.

An old man by this stage, Morgan continued to look towards
what the young could achieve. Before considering what he had
himself accomplished through a varied poetry of warning,
exhortation, exploration, remembrance and celebration, it is
worth looking briefly at his early life, when such achievement
must often have seemed unlikely. Growing up in Rutherglen
and Glasgow brought him into contact with aspects of life that
he would constantly return to in his writing. Then we can go
on to examine how the key concerns already mentioned – urban
life, political values, love, language, time and narrative – are
explored in particular poems, collections, translations and
theatrical works.

2. A POET'S LIFE

Growing up

Edwin Morgan was born on 27 April 1920 and grew up as an only child, with a sense of isolation and perhaps also of 'special-ness'. Born in Glasgow's West End, he stayed there and also in the well-off district of Pollokshields until he was about nine. Then the family moved to Burnside near Rutherglen where houses were cheaper. It was the period of the Depression, when industry declined in Scotland as elsewhere, with much poverty and unemployment. This had an impact on his father's work, but not because the family were particularly poor. Some websites show his father's occupation as a 'scrap-metal dealer'. In fact he was chief accountant for a substantial firm of ship-breakers and metal recyclers, Arnott, Young and Company. They had shipyards in Dalmuir on Clydeside and at Troon on the Ayrshire coast, as well as a deep-water facility on the island of Bute. The firm had been founded by Morgan's grand-father on his mother's side, who started out in the newly developing steelmaking industry of Lanarkshire and then saw the opportunities in recycling its raw materials. His mother had also worked as a secretary in her father's business before marriage.

As a child Edwin Morgan loved the sea and ships, and would have noticed the contrast between the family firm's ship-breaking activity and his own attraction to the freedom of sea voyages. Books of adventure and fantasy, including science fiction, offered an escape from daily life, but his curiosity and intelligence also drew him to general-knowledge magazines of science and exploration, to stamp-collecting and the making of scrap-books of interesting facts and pictures from scientific, zoological and archaeological developments. For a teenager growing up in favourable circumstances in the 1930s, this was an exciting decade of advances in jet propulsion, atomic research, radio astronomy, Kodachrome film and television. He was interested in words too, particularly unusual and foreign ones.

His parents were business people, clever but not at all interested in books. They were conservative, precise and

7

churchgoing, and careful about their son's moral education. They lacked any academic background and were rather disappointed by his choice of a career teaching English literature in Glasgow University. They would have preferred a more 'secure' job in banking or business. Morgan grew up with a rather nervous sense of being open to criticism, but learned to share their work ethic, determination, independence and concern for accuracy and achievement.

On his father's side of the family there were several influential factors. One was his deafness, which made communication difficult, especially since his son was so adept with language. Coming to terms with his father's misfortune possibly led to the focus in his poetry on the sound of words and breakdowns in communication. His father's own father had come from a non-industrial background: he was a 'silk-merchant' from Fife, trading in textiles. Morgan liked the hint of the exotic and far travel in that title. So his family heritage included both heavy industry and the imagined worlds of the Orient. There was some talk in his teenage years of his taking up an apprenticeship in the design department of Templeton's carpet factory in Glasgow, as he was good at art (although slightly colour-blind) and a very good draughtsman. He took Higher Art and might even have gone to art school, but language and literature won out in the end.

This artistic side was combined with an admiration for technology. His father's vivid descriptions of steelmaking and marine engines gave Morgan a positive appreciation of the modern industrial city that he never lost. He would later contrast this with the bleak view of cities shown by such modernist poets as T. S. Eliot. Glasgow was a heartland of heavy industry, in all its dirt, danger and physical effort, and for him it remained a powerful and ingenious place, even as the old industries declined and the city began to alter itself through slum clearance and road building. He was acutely aware of the impact of economic depression on the working conditions of his fellow Glaswegians, and became more socialist in his politics. He stopped going to church with his parents, and resisted his father's attempts to interest him in joining the Freemasons, a useful organisation for business networking. Besides English and French literature in his first year at university, he chose to study political economy, winning a prize for it, and also Russian. For him, economics and literature both dealt with values.

Glasgow shipbuilding at this period was a sectarian industry, and anti-Irish sentiment ran high. The family firm would never employ a Catholic. It is interesting that the great love relationship in Morgan's life was with a working-class Catholic, a store-man from industrial Lanarkshire who would certainly never have been offered a job in Arnott, Young and Company. That relationship began in the early 1960s. As a teenager in the 1930s, he had become aware that he was more attracted to boys in the class rather than to girls, and this puzzled him a great deal. The subject of sex was never discussed openly, and there were no books where he could find out about homosexuality. His parents were not satisfied with his results in mathematics at the local Rutherglen Academy, and entered him in a scholarship examination for the High School of Glasgow. As he travelled back and forth to school there by tram, he enjoyed listening to the passengers' dialect and humour, adding to the store of Scots expressions from Fife and Lanarkshire that his parents still used at home, and becoming 'bilingual'. The confident energy of his use of Scots in poems, translations and drama came from such early lived experience, as well as later study of historical dictionaries.

His day-to-day experience of having to pretend to be something that he was not, since his sexuality could not be openly expressed, probably also encouraged his later skill of writing in many voices or personae. But beginning his university studies in 1937 it was a source of guilt and confusion, and soon he found himself in love with two fellow students: Jean Watson, who was a very bright and strong-minded character, and Frank Mason, who was a Communist.

Going to war

The approach of war also caused him a great deal of conflict, as he was a pacifist by inclination. When called up for National Service in 1939, he almost became a conscientious objector but decided finally that the moral evil of Nazi Germany had to be fought. So he volunteered for the Royal Army Medical Corps, as a soldier but in a non-combatant role. After training in the Scottish Borders, his unit sailed out to Egypt via South Africa (the Mediterranean being by then too dangerous) to work in hospitals near the Suez Canal, and then in Lebanon and Palestine. He would not return home until 1945.

He had entered a different world of vivid impressions and new relationships, one that he would not address directly in poetry until much later in the 1970s. Yet that army experience shaped two of his earliest post-war publications: *The Cape of Good Hope* and *Beowulf* (both 1952). *Beowulf* was a translation of an Old English epic poem, in which a band of warriors voyage out to fight against the monster Grendel and his even more terrifying mother. Most university students found Old English a chore, but Morgan relished not only the complexity of its grammar and spelling but also the dauntless vision of life expressed in its poetry. Old English poets composed mainly for a male world of bonding, violence and honour. In the army now, having left his university textbooks behind, he found himself part of 'a band of brothers', enjoying the camaraderie and humour. He refused promotion so that he could remain as 'one of the boys'.

He came to see this *Beowulf* translation as his 'unwritten war poem' (as he described it in a new 2001 edition) with 'its themes of conflict and danger, voyaging and displacement, loyalty and loss'. Something of his feelings as a young soldier are expressed in the opening verse of 'The Unspoken' (p. 36), as the convoy rounds the Cape of Good Hope and a full moon rises:

> and we all crowded on to the wet deck, leaning on the rail, our
>   arms on each other's shoulders, gazing at the savage outcrop
>   of great Africa,
> And Tommy Cosh started singing 'Mandalay' and we joined in
>   with our raucous chorus of the unforgettable song [...]

The poet's wartime exultation is compared in this 1960s poem to his excited confusion of feelings at being part of history as he listened in the 1950s to the first radio messages sent from a Russian sputnik with a living creature, the small dog Laika, on board. Then both of these deep personal experiences are found to be less than the emotion of falling in love for the first time, with a depth that might remain 'unspoken' but not unwritten.

In the army Morgan had several homosexual affairs, risking court-martial, as well as positive friendships with heterosexual men. He would later evoke this period of his life in 'The New Divan' (1977), a hundred-stanza poem employing a glancing, disconnected 'Arabic' style of verse ('divan' is the Arabic word for such a sequence). Morgan's experience in the Middle East was partly one of living in history and prehistory, among the archaeological ruins of ancient cultures that had fascinated him since childhood. This is combined with memories of his work in the desert hospital, on sentry duty, as a stretcher-bearer, or in the operating theatre.

Return to Glasgow
Much soldiering is routine, of course. Morgan was far from the front line and worked mainly in hospital administration. Nevertheless, returning to civilian life in dark Glasgow after five years in the open Mediterranean air, he found it hard to readjust. He had decided to complete the final year and a half of his Honours degree, but came back as a different person. Romantic poetry was particularly difficult, since it bore so little relation to the army life he had just left. However, he eventually got back into the way of studying, made friends with younger students, and graduated with the second-highest degree in the whole Faculty of Arts. He was offered a lecturing post in the English Department at Glasgow University, and remained there until retirement in 1980 as a professor, respected teacher and mentor to many Scottish poets in the new generation.

He stayed on in his parents' house until he finally bought his own flat in the early 1960s after he turned forty. They offered continuity and company during what was a troubled period in his life. His opportunities to write poetry were limited to the university vacations, because of the amount of teaching and assessment involved in his term-time work.

More worrying was the fact that his own early poetry was
often rejected by literary journals, which regularly preferred
his translations from Old English, Italian, Russian and
French. He translated Petrarchan love poetry from Renaissance Italy and France, with its emphasis on unattainable
and ideal love. Morgan had much personal experience of this,
since he had no partner and his relationships were a series
of casual affairs, often with working-class men, sometimes
involving violence. That way of life was vividly described in
his poem 'Glasgow Green', which he came to see as a plea
for 'gay liberation' before that phrase even existed: 'And how
shall these men live? / Providence, watch them go! / Watch
them love and watch them die!' (p. 31).

He was also dismayed in the 1950s by the nuclear arms
race. Here was a perversion of science by politics, that risked
destroying everything individual, curious, and distinctive
about life as it has evolved on earth. The poem which opens
New Selected Poems is the stern 'Stanzas of the Jeopardy'
(p. 9) from his 1952 collection *Dies Irae*, the day of God's wrath.
More precisely, in the atomic brinksmanship of the Cold War
with Russia, this is the day of man's self-destruction. Every
single thing itemised by the poet in loving detail – railway
sidings, dancers, children 'speaking to the wind and stars in
a dream', badger, hedgehog, 'Lovers lying in the dunes of
summer, swimmers / Flashing like sudden fire in the bay –':
everything

> Shall craze to an intolerable blast
> And hear at midnight the very end of the world.

What made such matters even more personal was Morgan's
admiration for the Russian spirit, as encountered through
translating many of its more experimental poets, and his
support too for the attempt to build a socialist society. Although
never a Communist Party member, he followed the post-war
progress of the USSR closely, and took part in a month's study
tour there in May 1955, organised by the Scotland–USSR
Friendship Society. He was struck by the contrast between
the drab outward appearance of things and the happiness of

the people, and captivated by the sheer energy of rebuilding that went on day and night. It was the same sort of revolutionary energy that he responded to in the poetry of Vladimir Mayakovsky (1893–1930). His translations of Mayakovsky and other socialist poets in the small collection *Sovpoems* (1961) would be a breakthrough for him in various ways, leading into the most productive decade of his life.

Many of the poems for which Morgan is best known were written in the 1960s, so it is time to move from his early life to the poems that, for him, revealed its true purpose and meaning. Writing an encouraging letter to the Scottish poet Robin Fulton in the mid-1970s, he described how in the 1950s life 'dragged its black claws' through his own bleak mid-thirties years, which were then transformed in his early forties – 'it was like being shot from a gun'. That exhilarating energy carried his poetry forward through the 1960s and beyond, in a fusillade of small-press pamphlets, poetry collections and special editions, critical essays, edited volumes and journals, reviews, translations, a film script and his first opera libretto.

Morgan gave frequent readings of his poetry in the UK and overseas. He enjoyed all cities which had a vibrant street-life, with Naples, New York, Cairo and Istanbul being particular favourites. But he always came back to Glasgow. There is a pattern of voyage and return in his life as in his poetry. He wrote, taught, lived and died within the same familiar West End patch where he was born. This allowed his imagination to roam freely to the farthest reaches, while also keeping a sharp eye on the daily life and stresses of a modern city.

3. A POET'S CHOICE

Variations on a theme

Opening the *New Selected Poems* we might be surprised by the biblical imagery in its first three poems. Morgan is not usually associated with religion, unlike, say, George Mackay Brown. The anti-war poem 'Stanzas of the Jeopardy' ends with a prophetic warning: 'As you receive these verses, O Corinthians'. It is as if in his anguish at the thought of atomic destruction he reverts to the bible-based preaching rhetoric that he had rejected in his teens. Perhaps he is signalling that his poetry early and late would have the most serious of intentions. This poem is immediately contrasted by 'Verses for a Christmas Card' (p. 11) which takes the Christian season as a starting point. But there is nothing trite or familiar about this Christmas message:

> This endyir starnacht blach and klar
> As I on Cathkin-fells held fahr
> A snaepuss fussball showerdown
> With nezhny smirl and whirlcome rown
> Upon my pollbare underlift,
> And smazzled all my gays with srift [...]

What is going on here? Well, the poet takes a walk through the snowy woodland of Cathkin Braes near his parents' Rutherglen home and some snow dislodging from a tree falls on his upturned head. But there is also a hint of artistic ambition in the language, and perhaps of self-display. The multi-levelled punning style of James Joyce's *Finnegans Wake* (1939) fascinated him, as did the inventive poetic language of Gerard Manley Hopkins (1844–1889), whose work he first read in his teens in the *Faber Book of Modern Verse* (1936). He identified strongly with this Jesuit priest, in his isolation, his troubled sexuality and his burdensome work in nineteenth-century Liverpool and Glasgow parishes and later in University College, Dublin. So here the young Morgan is setting forth his own talent in distinguished literary company. The poem appeared in the locally published collection *The Vision of Cathkin Braes*

(1952), and the word 'gays' (in the last line quoted above) did not then have its widely current meaning of homosexual. But other poems in the collection, such as the rollicking 'Vision' of the collection's title, do hint at sexual activity on Cathkin Braes, so this aspect of the poet's identity is also present.

The following poem in *New Selected Poems* is 'Message Clear' (p. 12), which combines a religious challenge with an arresting form of concrete poetry invented by Morgan: the 'emergent poem'. This form draws its meanings from a powerful or well-known quotation – in this case Christ's words in St John's Gospel, 5. 25: 'I am the resurrection and the life'. The poem extracts significant permutations from the letters in that sentence (for example, 'i am here / i act / i run / i meet / i stand / i tie / i am thoth / i am ra'). It spreads the letters that make these statements out along each line to match their location in the final phrase, printed in full at the foot of the poem, in which all the meanings rest. The technique is rather like codebreaking, finding hidden information or significance, such as the link made in the quotation above between Christ and the ancient Egyptian gods, Thoth and Ra. The reading of the biblical phrase is made more halting and problematic, but also more thought-provoking. What does each of these broken sentences mean, and what might they be suggesting about how Jesus understood his own life and death?

The context of the poem suggests that this was more than just playing with words, as some critics complained when it was first published. It was composed on a bus journey home from the hospital where Morgan's father lay dying of cancer. So there is a sense of the poet exploring the meaning of his father's suffering, his approaching death and his traditional Christian beliefs. The poem 'emerges' from clumsy, broken speech (we remember his deafness) towards an increasing affirmation. Against the seeming meaninglessness of death it asserts the power of life, and of the questioning mind, and of the fascinating energy of Jesus in the Gospel, realising his full identity.

By beginning his own selection of poems with these three variations on the theme of religion, all in markedly different styles, Morgan may be preparing his readers for the sheer

variety to come. With this poet, we should not expect a single
viewpoint. Rather, the same topics are revisited from different
angles. The poetry will be as varied as humanity.

Concrete poetry

'Message Clear' introduces a series of ten concrete poems,
dated 1966 to 1969. Morgan was interested in the concrete
poetry movement because it was new, avant-garde, international and also intellectually engaging. As a teacher of the
traditional canon of English and Scottish poetry, he was
intrigued by the theoretical writing emerging from this movement, particularly from the brothers Haroldo and Augusto de
Campos in São Paulo, Brazil, and from Eugen Gomringer in
Switzerland. He often gave talks with slide illustrations to
analyse what was happening to the eye and mind in the act
of reading, when confronted by these strange new texts. Of
the British concrete poets, Edwin Morgan and Ian Hamilton
Finlay were among the best-known internationally. Both Scots
had positive links with other artists and writers interested in
exploring this interface between image, sound and meaning,
and between words, sculpture and kinetic art.

Morgan's approach to concrete poetry shows clear links to
his other concerns. For instance, 'Archives' (p. 14) follows the
phrase 'generation upon / generation upon / generation upon
[...]' down through the ages and eras towards the foot of the
page, until the phrase increasingly loses coherence and breaks
up, just as recorded history becomes misremembered or reduced
to archaeological fragments. So this poem can be seen as part
of the poet's exploration of time. Although it was sometimes
claimed that concrete poetry was too playful to deal with
serious political issues, 'Starryveldt' (p. 15) tackles the 1960
Sharpeville massacre in the South African Transvaal, when
white police shot sixty-nine black demonstrators. The poem
takes the 's' and 'v' sounds of the township's name Sharpeville
as a refrain, transposed into flashing imagery ('shriekvolley'
... 'spoorvengeance' ... 'spadevoice') and spits out an angry
litany in which the word 'strive' becomes more and more
insistent. It ends in capitals: 'SO: VAEVICTIS', which means
'woe to the vanquished ones', or 'the conquered have no rights'.

But this is not just an elegy for the dead Africans. The momentum of this protest poem leads towards a sense of inevitable reversal, in which present-day oppressors can expect no forgiveness.

'The Computer's First Christmas Card' (p. 16) works more cheerfully through Morgan's interest not just in engineering technology but in the potential of 'information technology'. That phrase had not been invented when the poem was written, and computers were as clumsy as this one appears to be as it batters its way towards a seasonal greeting. Morgan was on his university's Computing Committee, which discussed the possible impact of these new machines across the curriculum, but poetically he was most interested in Russian experiments in machine translation, where the results were patchy but nevertheless intriguing. The poem works by a repeated pattern of phrases with Christmas connotations but unusual collocations, using a binary system as computers do:

```
j o l l y m e r r y
h o l l y b e r r y
j o l l y b e r r y
m e r r y h o l l y
```

and so on. The spaced letters have the look of the punchcards that were used in early computers as simple programs. Or they might simply be a narrow printout, ending with the mistaken flourish: MERRYCHR / YSANTHEMUM.

Morgan's interests in language and translation also figure in 'Siesta of a Hungarian Snake' (p. 15):

s sz sz SZ sz SZ sz ZS zs ZS zs zs zs z

Hungarian was one of his favourite languages because of its difficulty and unique linguistic features. Here the poem takes the 'sz' letter combination frequently found in Hungarian, and relates it to the letters seen in children's comics above snoozing characters. This snake is like a comic rattlesnake in the Spanish–American desert (hence the 'siesta' of the title) dozing after a meal, as seen by the girth of capitals round the middle

of its length. It is done very adeptly, the poet's ingenuity nicely
engaged by the compression of the form.

But concrete poetry was also capable of an artistic credo.
'Opening the Cage' (p. 17) takes its starting point in fourteen
words by the American composer and musical theorist John
Cage, whose 1952 composition *4'33"* explored the 'silence' of
environmental sounds accompanying a performance in which
the musicians do not play a note for four minutes and thirty-
three seconds. Morgan takes Cage's fourteen-word phrase 'I
have nothing to say and I am saying it and that is poetry'
(from his 'Lecture on Nothing', 1949) and uses it for a set of
fourteen variations:

> I have to say poetry and is that nothing and am I saying it
> I am and I have poetry to say and is that nothing saying it
> I am nothing and I have poetry to say and that is saying it
> I that am saying poetry have nothing and it is I and to say

and so on until the final variation: 'Saying poetry is nothing and
to that I say I am and have it' – a statement of competence
and confidence, expressing the lively optimism of those 1960s
years. The 'I am' echoes the other 'I am' of 'Message Clear',
but in a more personal context of artistic experimentation.
Are these fourteen lines, in some sense, a challenge to traditional poetry, as exemplified in the fourteen-line sonnet form?
He certainly cuts Cage's original phrase short, and draws
attention to the figure fourteen in a subtitle: '*14 variations on
14 words*'. Once he had broken with tradition in verse, however,
as Cage had in music, Morgan would return to the sonnet
form afresh in *Glasgow Sonnets* (1972) and *Sonnets from
Scotland* (1984).

His optimism here was a response to the mood of the 1960s,
with changes in music, fashion and political values among
young people in many countries seeming to signal a new radical
awakening after the austere and conservative 1950s. At a
personal level, it was also a response to love, and so his concrete
selection includes a poem referring both to the Beatles' music
and to the new experience of being in love. The title 'Strawberry
Fields Forever' (p. 13) echoes the Lennon/McCartney song.

Isolated words are then spread across the page in a puzzling way: 'my blackie', 'losing', 'smirr', 'whistle', 'kneedeep'. Writing to Geoffrey Summerfield, a lecturer and editor who helped to popularise Morgan's poetry in influential Penguin school anthologies, he explained something of the poem's background:

> I imagine two lovers drifting through dewy fields of long grass – walking apart, coming together again, as the fall of the words down the page is meant to indicate – nature is mysterious but vivid all round them as in Hardy or Lawrence – the dewdrops, the slight 'smirr' of rain, the suggestion of foxes, the hazel-tree, the blackbird ('blackie' the usual Scots term for it) whistling – and I think from this you'll be able to get on to the words 'losing' and 'patter' which have more than one meaning/reference [...]. It is, of course, associated in my mind with the Lennon/McCartney song, which has always haunted me [...].

Although concrete poetry was accused at the time of being cold and clinical in its obsessive manipulation of words, Morgan knew that it was capable of a whole range of tones, and that he preferred the light and warm end of that spectrum. We can also see from these examples that it could carry forward his thematic concerns with politics, love, language and so forth. It also relates to his enthusiasm for engineering and technology, because in his concrete poems he is working out how the component parts of poetry fit together as in a well-designed machine – the visual elements of print size and layout meshing with the vocal elements of repetition, alliteration, rhythm and rhyme – to create a clear yet intriguing message.

Although concrete poetry was a relatively short-lived movement which began to break apart in the 1970s along theoretical or national lines, he was able to take the lessons learned from its practice into his later mainstream collections. For example, *From Glasgow to Saturn* (1973) has 'The Loch Ness Monster's Song', 'The First Men on Mercury' and 'Spacepoem 3: Off Course' (pp. 66, 69, 70); and *The New Divan* (1977) has 'Shaker Shaken' (p. 101), based on the early American charismatic religious practice of glossolalia, or speaking in tongues. We might say that concrete poetry presented him with the chance to teach himself to speak in radically different tongues, and that he never forgot this lesson even when he moved on into other forms.

The Second Life (1968)

Morgan's breakthrough collection was *The Second Life* (1968), published by Edinburgh University Press. Given his versatility and productivity, it is surprising to think that he was nearly fifty before gaining wide recognition in Scotland. It would take a further five years to establish his reputation in England. This was another form of isolation that he felt quite keenly. Having no single or recognisable style probably made him difficult for readers and publishers to feel comfortable with. His work was certainly increasingly published, but often in journals catering to fairly exclusive sets of readerships: avant-garde experimentalists; enthusiasts for East European poetry in translation; those who recognised a gay perspective; enthusiasts for the Beat poetry of 1950s America; those who responded to his urban concerns.

Within Scotland, there were very few literary publishers, and even fewer willing to risk the losses that poetry collections often involved. There was also opposition towards urban, experimental and, indeed, Glaswegian writing. The most influential Scottish poet of the time, Hugh MacDiarmid (1892–1978), great poet and socialist as he was, had little time for the crowds, poverty and dirty industrial life of Scotland's largest city, or for its dialect. MacDiarmid's earlier poetic use of Lowland Scots language (sometimes called 'synthetic' or 'plastic' Scots because he brought together words from different eras and regions) had been mainly based on rural dialects. His example had been followed by other Scottish poets. He also disliked the way that American experimental and Beat writers such as Allen Ginsberg, Jack Kerouac and William Burroughs, or Scottish avant-garde figures such as Alexander Trocchi (1925–1984), were associated with drug culture, homosexuality or both. A famous public quarrel took place between MacDiarmid and Trocchi at the Edinburgh Festival Writers' Conference in August 1962. Morgan was on the platform on that occasion, arguing against MacDiarmid for a more urban Scots language, closer to the actual speech of everyday people, and for a more outward-looking, international perspective. Although he understood the totality of MacDiarmid's achievement better than most, praising the later 'difficult' and scientific poetry as much as the magical early lyrics in Scots, Morgan rejected any narrowly traditional or inward-looking approach to language as a badge of Scottish identity.

Perhaps for this defiant reason, *The Second Life* opens with poems that are American in style and content. 'The Old Man and the Sea' evokes the suicide by gunshot of the novelist Ernest Hemingway, and 'The Death of Marilyn Monroe' raises questions posed by the film star's death from a drug overdose (pp. 20–21). Both are written in a free-ranging American style, influenced by the sprawling 'democratic' poetry of Walt Whitman (1819–1892) whom Morgan admired, and the spoken energy of Allen Ginsberg. These two elegies for artists probe America's relationship with violence, and its elevation and then destruction of heroic figures. The poems question the psychological and cultural cost of a relentless hunting after success. Morgan's earlier serious moral style on social issues is now moderated by engagement with the loss of individual talent, and also by bringing a humane and Scottish perspective to bear on another culture. The opening sentence of 'The Old Man and the Sea' stretches for nineteen lines, suggesting the remorseless approach of the death-like white mist, and draws us into the moment of despairing suicide. In 'The Death of Marilyn Monroe', a series of questions and exclamations is used to make the case against a star system that destroyed this 'child of America'. The post-war cultural supremacy of the United States through media and the arts is mirrored back upon itself through the desolation of two of its most celebrated performers.

Scotland too is presented in mirror-image, as 'Canedolia' (p. 23). The subtitle 'An Off-Concrete Scotch Fantasia' may be a mischievous gesture towards mainstream Scottish poets who had denigrated Morgan's experimental work. It is partly a sound poem, in fact, with a gossipy comic dialogue playing off against the onomatopoeia or suggestiveness of actual

place-names from Gaelic, Norse, Anglian and Pictish roots.
It is not only a funny poem in performance, but also neatly
expresses a peculiarly Scottish tension between the most
depressing aspects of this country and culture ('shiskine,
scrabster, and snizort') and the often astonishing beauty of
its clear light: 'blinkbonny! airgold! thundergay!'. That last
word might suggest again some sly sexual subtext in the
goings-on of the inhabitants of this not-quite-Scotland: 'we
foindle and fungle, we bonkle and meigle ... and there's aye
a bit of tilquhilly'. Overall, a good-humoured atmosphere of
carnival runs through this praise-poem for a whole country
and its named communities, leaving us uplifted by a final
toast – appropriately the name of a mountain: 'schiehallion!
schiehallion! schiehallion!'.

'Good Friday' and other Glasgow poems

The Second Life alternated brief sequences of concrete and
other experimental work with longer themed sections of poems
on Glasgow, love and science fiction. The set of Glasgow poems
was particularly new, for the poet as well as for his readers.

   The Glaswegian working-class speech rhythms found in
'Good Friday' (p. 26) were more unexpected in poetry in the
1960s than they would be today. That was the language of
variety theatre or pantomime, but not what you would expect
to hear in a poem, especially not one called 'Good Friday' that
opens with a reference to the hour of the crucifixion of Jesus:
'Three o'clock'. But this is a city scene and a local voice, with
the bus route, the street name, the slightly slurred speech and
clumsy movements of a man who has 'had a wee drink': 'D's
this go –' / he flops beside me – 'right along Bath Street?'. Even
the line-breaks at the start seem to enact the lurching movement of the bus, as the meaning swings from one line to the
next in an ungainly but realistic way.

   Neither Morgan nor his parents drove a car, so travel by
tram and bus brought the poet into close proximity with the
lives and language of ordinary people. He liked the way that
Glaswegians will often start up a conversation with strangers
(visitors to the city often comment on this). He liked the lively
language that they used, and had a poet's accurate ear for its

phrasing and dialectal usages, so that the drunk man's speech rings true. This was where Morgan disagreed with MacDiarmid, as we have seen. 'Good Friday' shows what the more traditionalist Scots-language poets were missing.

Whereas some people fear the Glaswegian habit of interaction and direct address, and disapprove of Glasgow's hard-drinking culture and sectarian divisions, Morgan responds with sympathy to the man's humanity – to his uncertainty of direction (both factually and spiritually), his recognition of being trapped by his lack of education, his generosity to his family. In some social situations it is considered bad manners to discuss religion and social class differences, but here in Glasgow the topics are raised directly, and without antagonism. There is also something to admire – the man is a survivor, as once again the verse rhythms and line-breaks take him swinging down the stairs of the bus and off at his stop. Unsteady legs, which the final line-breaks mimic, won't stop him on his ordinary mission of kindness. He has not spent all of his money on drink, and he knows where he is going: to buy Easter eggs for his grandchildren. The poet sets this ancient folk custom, and uncertain religious awareness, and perhaps some political sense of social need or of working-class lives unfulfilled, against the drunk man's honesty. And it is the personality that shines through.

Morgan's poems of Glasgow life soon became well-known, since they were accessible and timely in a period of major social changes, not only in Glasgow but in other cities. New road systems, slum clearance, bright high-rise flats and dispersal of families from the packed inner city altered the appearance of smoke-stained Glasgow and held out new hope, especially for the young. Mistakes were made in design, it is true, and some building materials finally failed the test of Scottish weather. Moreover, an older way of life was irreversibly changing along with community identities, and Morgan found himself torn between optimism and regret. It was the artist's duty to record this change. In 'To Joan Eardley' (p. 25) he praises the way the painter has caught 'a blur of children / at their games' beside a now-demolished sweetshop in Glasgow's Rottenrow:

Such rags and streaks
that master us! –
that fix what the pick
and bulldozer have crumbled
to a dingier dust,
the living blur
fiercely guarding
energy that has vanished [...]

Morgan owned four paintings by Joan Eardley (1921–1963)
and admired her determination to catch that 'living blur' of
change in city streets and seascapes, alongside the energy of
those who had made a life there.

He, too, tried to fulfil this artistic duty towards his city's
story, as in 'King Billy' (p. 29). Here he records the older
Glasgow of razor fights between gangs founded on sectarian
lines, now brought back into focus by the death of gang-leader
Billy Fullerton in 1962. At its peak in the early 1930s, his
gang of 'Billy Boys' had many hundreds of members, and their
aim was to maintain Protestant dominance at street level in
a city with a large population of Catholics, mainly of Irish
immigrant extraction. Their fights would have made newspaper headlines when Morgan was in his early teens, and
indeed the poem uses a form of reportage, almost like a
newsreel scenario: 'Grey over Riddrie the clouds piled up, /
dragged their rain through the cemetery trees'. The thirteen-
line unfinished sentence that opens the second stanza plays
out the funeral scene, with flashback memories intercut ('the
word, the scuffle, the flash, the shout / bloody crumpling in
the close / bricks for papish windows [...]'). It is powerfully
done.

In its contrasting images from the life of 'King Billy', early
and late, and of former gang members marching in respectful
procession to the hymn 'Onward Christian Soldiers', played
now with 'unironic lips' by Orange flute bands normally used
to assert the rightness of Protestant–Unionist supremacy,
Morgan complicates both the life story and the legend. He
leaves us with a parting challenge in the final lines: 'Deplore
what is to be deplored / and then find out the rest'. What

remains most vividly, perhaps, is the dripping red, white and blue wreath, pricked out with gold: 'To Our Leader of Thirty Years Ago'. Exploring a culture that might be outdated and pitiful, he conveys a sense that the greater pity was in the poverty (both social and spiritual) of a Scottish working-class life that could find no better leader than this violent street-fighter. In reflecting on one legend, Morgan also brings another still-persistent media half-truth into question: the violent Glasgow of *No Mean City* (1935) with its Gorbals hardmen and razor gangs.

'Glasgow Green' (p. 30) is another call for greater under-standing. Morgan was surprised that the poem got published, but then surprised again to find that its content had not fully registered with many readers. Or if it had, there was no discus-sion of it. Here is another dark Glasgow underworld, also violent. The poem presents a haunting scene of gay men meeting at night in the unlit spaces of Glasgow Green by the River Clyde. It is all the more disturbing because only half-seen or half-surmised – 'All shadows are alive' – and the eerie emphasis is on sounds from the darkness: 'cough', 'mutter', 'whispers'. Although it is a scene of rape, 'there's no crying for help'. The poet is a witness, or even a victim: 'the sweat / is real, the wrestling under a bush / is real, the dirty starless river / is the real Clyde [...]'.

This is contrasted with the clean and morning world of family life, when Glasgow Green returns to its main function as a drying green where mothers from crowded slums peg out clean sheets and clothes, while their children play nearby. In his determination to make a case for those excluded from such a life, as he himself was, Morgan returns to a biblical resonance in the imagery of 'thorn in the flesh', 'wilderness', 'water' and 'seed'. He asserts that here too there is a harvest, if it could be recognised. If there is a wilderness, then it should be watered and reclaimed. The sheets 'blow and whip in the sunlight', but the stark contrast of night and day reminds us that the norm for many is not available to all: 'the beds of married love / are islands in a sea of desire'. The park will become a place of instability again when night falls, with men afloat like drift-wood there.

Morgan was able to observe his city in many moods, with an unusual blend of almost dispassionate detail combined with a sense of pity or tenderness. 'In the Snack-bar' (p. 32) is a clear example of this, as the description moves from the image of the blind hunchback 'in his stained beltless gaberdine / like a monstrous animal caught in a tent / in some story', towards contact with the person through his halting speech and need of a helping hand ('Give me – your arm – it's better'), so that, drawn close, the poet must 'concentrate / my life to his: crunch of spilt sugar, slidy puddle from the night's umbrellas [...]'. So he learns to see how the blind man 'sees', through other senses. Their joint progress is slowly and patiently enacted, downstairs to the toilet and then back up again ('He climbs, we climb') and the poet recognises in him the 'persisting patience of the undefeated / which is the nature of man when all is said'. This is the same persistence that an artist needs, a scientist or an explorer. A sense of their shared human qualities, however, cannot erase 'his strangeness / under his mountainous coat'. The poet knows that this man's life 'depends on many who would evade him'. There is perhaps an outsider's sense of identification with the blind man's world of darkness: 'and yet he must trust men'. The poem's ending catches a complex ambiguity of feelings: compassion, horror at the man's fate, half-admiration for the way he hauls his burden of a body forward. Is the last line a prayer, a reflection or an expletive? 'Dear Christ, to be born for this!'

Morgan loved Glasgow's variousness. Those darker moods can immediately be countered by its people's energy. 'Trio' (p. 34) is a perfect example, set at the cold end of a winter's day but sparking with life and celebration. In the happy trio of two women and one man each carries something simple yet precious – a new guitar decorated with tinsel and a sprig of mistletoe, a baby in a white shawl, a Chihuahua in a Royal Stewart tartan coat. The poet catches the scene's joy and significance, which is not necessarily Christian (these folk speak like ordinary Glaswegians, not Magi) but harks back to pagan times, with the 'Orphean sprig' of mistletoe recalling the price paid by Orpheus to enter Hades to rescue his wife Eurydice. In their laughter, careless energy and gift-giving the three embody new life, and it seems that neither fate nor negativity can stand against them: 'Monsters of the year / go blank, are scattered back, / can't bear this march of three'.

'The Starlings in George Square' (Glasgow's main civic square) also opens on an evening scene as the starlings swoop down to roost: 'like a shower of arrows they cross / the flash of a western window, / they bead the wires with jet [...]' (p. 27). We focus in on one man and his wide-eyed son, the man pointing up and smiling to the boy who, watching the swooping arcs of birds, feels 'a stab of confused sweetness' that pierces him 'like a story, / a story more than a song'. This sounds autobiographical in its detail, and is reminiscent of Morgan's introduction to his own poems in the school anthology *Worlds: Seven Modern Poets* (1974). There he talks about 'the poetry before poetry', in his memory of songs sung at home and records played, the adults dealing cards and smoking – the feeling that he would remember the scene forever, as with the wheeling starlings now: 'He will never forget that evening'.

The poem is in three sections. The second takes off into comic misunderstandings as the chirping of the starlings makes normal communication impossible. The last section reflects on communication too, but more ruefully. Measures taken to prevent the starlings from landing and depositing on civic buildings and statues mean that we will lose the chance ever to 'decipher that sweet frenzied whistling'. This is Morgan's love of language again, and his sense of the necessary relationship of all living things. We should adjust ourselves to them, as they do to our hard grey roofs and buttresses: 'They like the warm cliffs of man'.

Love poems

The love poems that Morgan was writing at this time gain depth from the way in which changes in the poet's emotional life paralleled developments in the city. Again the movement is one from darkness into light, from a constrained and impoverished half-life into the promise of a clean start. 'The Second Life' (p. 35) gives its title to the whole collection, and opens with a description that blends Glasgow and New York: 'and the winter moon flooding the skyscrapers, northern – / an aspiring place, glory of the bridges, foghorns / are enormous messages'. Everything has its voice and language in this poet's world, and his own rhythms reply with an excitement carried on the connectives and dashes. Glasgow is being remade. Writing in his new flat 'as the aircraft roar / over building sites, in this warm west light [...]' he notes crowded daffodil banks and the green of May but also:

> [...] the slow great blocks rising
> under yellow tower cranes, concrete and glass and steel
> out of a dour rubble it was and barefoot children gone –

Thinking back to winter nights, he recalls the flash of skaters on nearby Bingham's Pond, lit by car headlights, then the ice breaking up and painted boats coming out on the water, 'ready for pleasure. [...] Black oar cuts a glitter: it is heaven on earth'. Then, as often in Morgan's poetry, there is a reflective turn towards the changes brought around by time. Like a seed emerging out of darkness, like a grey snakeskin sloughed so that a shining one appears, like the shrugging off of a city's coat of grime, like a declaration of love after fearful silence – all that we had grown accustomed to can be discarded, as this second life awakens, for the poet and his city: 'Slip out of the darkness: it is time'.

In this new city, he learns to see and sense differently. In 'From a City Balcony' (p. 38) he recalls wandering with his lover in Glen Fruin 'with butterflies and cuckoos', and contrasts the witnesses there ('a sparkling burn, white lambs, the blaze of gorse [...] and then the witness was my hand closing on yours') with the busy traffic passing along the road below. Those drivers cannot see who it is on the balcony, pouring such joy of remembrance that 'It brims, it spills over and over / down to the parched earth and the relentless wheels'.

'Strawberries' (p. 39) blends sensuality and tenderness, an ordinary occasion skilfully unfolded in brief plain lines to make it, in the light of emotion, extraordinary. And 'One Cigarette' (p. 40) again takes an ordinary sense and complicates it – 'Is it smell, is it taste?' – until it is the smoke that, human-like, lies back in the dark, and the ash sighs down in the ashtray.

A non-smoker, Morgan finds an erotic charge in the smoke left behind: 'You are here again, and I am drunk on your tobacco lips'. The smoke communicates, being a 'signal' or message of the power of love, inhaled with the very air we breathe.

Science fiction poems

Morgan's interest in contemporary rocket technology and space exploration combined easily with his childhood love of adventure stories with strongly imagined settings, shading towards fantasy and science fiction. Edgar Rice Burroughs, Jules Verne, Edgar Allan Poe and H. G. Wells were among his favourite authors. Space exploration also took forward the idea of a close-knit group of adventurers, rather like the Old English war bands which attracted him. Those were mainly male, but contemporary astronauts were not exclusively so, as the Russians included women cosmonauts from an early stage.

The Second Life contained two contrasting science fiction poems, one set in the future and one in the past – a reminder, perhaps, that for Morgan the great unexplored mystery was not space but time. 'In Sobieski's Shield' (p. 41) is named after the fifth-smallest constellation in the northern sky, called 'Scutum Sobiescianum' (Sobieski's Shield) by the Polish astronomer Johannes Hevelius in 1684. John III Sobieski, King of Poland, was famed as a military hero for breaking the Ottoman siege of Vienna in 1683 with a much smaller force. The poem's title is well chosen, for it is a disturbing narrative of war and its aftermath. It opens with a breathless unpunctuated narrative of chaos on earth, as the sun fails to rise. One plan to preserve earthly life is to dematerialise human beings and then rematerialise them on a planet that might support life, near a sun in Sobieski's Shield.

The speaker has been chosen for this mission, with his wife and son. The technology for the process is uncertain, and part of the fascination of the poem comes from the speaker's combination of scientific observation of the changes wrought on himself and his family by the process they have gone through: his wife's 'strange and beautiful crown of bright red hair', his own four-fingered hand and his son's one nipple. This is combined with tenderness as he watches his wife come alive

into 'her second life'. The setting is a 'harsh metallic plain /
that belches cobalt from its craters under a / white-bronze
pulsing gong of a sun [...]'. These craters are suddenly transposed into images of trench warfare from the First World War,
and the scientist is shaken to see the hand of a dead soldier
reaching up from a waterlogged crater, with a tattooed heart
still visible on his arm. He is even more shocked to find that
a fragment of memory has branded his own arm with a similar
heart-shaped birthmark:

> The rematerialisation has picked up these fragments I have
> a graft of war and ancient agony forgive
> me my dead helper

It is a moving moment as this undemonstrative man fiercely
hugs his wife and child, realising 'that we are bound to all
that lived' but must, with this understanding, look not to the
past but to the future. The poem ends with a new beginning:
they leave the shelter of their protective dome to prospect for
whatever this seemingly hostile environment will offer – a
second chance of life. For Morgan, Milton was the greatest
English poet, and the ending of his *Paradise Lost*, as Adam
and Eve make their way from the Garden out into the world,
was a supreme achievement. Something of that mood is present
in the final lines of 'In Sobieski's Shield'. We can also see the
modern poet exploring variations on the theme of 'the second
life', deepening the perspectives offered by his collection as a
whole. Here it is future science and not religion that offers
resurrection and a new life, albeit only on difficult terrain
where survival will demand from these survivors as much
human effort and ingenuity as our present planet has cost
over the generations.

'From the Domain of Arnheim' (p. 44) takes us back in time.
The title comes from Morgan's past also, when he studied art
at school. 'The Domain of Arnheim' (1847) was the title of a
short story by Edgar Allan Poe. It was also the inspiration in
1938 of the first of a series of paintings by René Magritte, the
surrealist artist, responding to Poe's description of a landscape
uniting 'beauty, magnificence and strangeness', one improved

by human intervention to resemble 'the handiwork of the angels that hover between man and God'. The aim of such prodigious landscaping in the story was to bring humans closer to those higher beings.

The poem opens with an unfinished statement of the time-travellers' aim in undertaking the voyage – it is as if the speed of the flight leaves their plans adrift, and so it proves. They immediately arrive on an ice-field in the domain of Arnheim, which appears to be on earth during one of the Ice Ages. The two travellers move arm in arm down the slippery ice-slope towards the fires of a prehistoric settlement, where the people seem to be celebrating the birth of a child, with song and dancing, drums and trumpets. Like ghosts or angels the travellers can be sensed but not seen: 'To them we were a displacement of the air / a sudden chill, yet we had no power / over their fear'. The fear is equalled by the courage of one man:

> A sweating trumpeter took
> a brand from the fire with a shout and threw it
> where our bodies would have been –
> we felt nothing but his courage.

The travellers get back to the mothership, but are themselves haunted by the man's bravery, which somehow holds more significance than any samples collected on the voyage: 'From time the souvenirs are deeds'. The poem is dramatic and powerful in its opposition of two cultures, where the more sophisticated are moved by their own intrusion into a different world. The realisation is held in tension at the centre of the poem as the lines shorten:

> What had we stopped
> but joy?
> I know you felt
> the same dismay, you gripped my arm, they were waiting
> for what they knew of us to pass.

This physical contact and shared emotion between the voyagers points towards a shared 'humanity' recognisable across time. They can understand and admire the act of courage that follows, which somehow promises the ultimate survival of these people.

The Second Life was an artistic success and firmly established Morgan's position as a leading Scottish poet. It won an Arts Council Award, and sold well. Its design was quite radical, not only in the range of its content and styles but also in its squarish shape (to cope with the layout of some of the concrete poetry) and striking yellow cover. It was also typeset using a computer, although this untried approach suffered from breakdowns and delays. At this time, Morgan was not only teaching full-time but co-editing *Scottish Poetry*, an annual volume of new writing, and the quarterly arts and current affairs journal *Scottish International*, as well as reviewing and translating for various publications. His intellectual energy was prodigious: 'like being shot from a gun', as he said – or a rocket.

There was also the positive sense of fascination with life's variety. As he describes it in 'A View of Things' (p. 46):

what I love about dormice is their size
what I hate about rain is its sneer
what I love about the Bratach Gorm is its unflappability
what I hate about scent is its smell
what I love about newspapers is their etaoin shrdl ...

And so on through a further twenty-two loves and hates. But we feel that he loves most of it, really – or loves the witty form of the poem and the chance to make us think about our own idiosyncratic preferences. We might need to look up the Bratach Gorm ('The Blue Banner'), which is the top prize in a London bagpiping competition, and puzzle over the newspaper misprint (more common in those days of hot-metal typesetting) which seems as if it should mean something. Some of its anagrams are 'darn hostile', 'hotel drains' or 'hairnet sold', though none seems right. Perhaps the point of the poem is to make us pause for a while over such oddities.

4. GAINS, LOSSES

Poems of the 1970s

The 1970s, Morgan would later claim, were a blank compared with his marvellous 1960s. What he probably meant was that there was plenty to blank out, notably the deaths of four people who meant a great deal to him. He was present when his mother died of a stroke in April 1970, on the day after his fiftieth birthday. In 1975 Veronica Forrest-Thomson, a very bright experimental poet from Glasgow with whom he had corresponded since her last years at school, died of a drug overdose at the age of twenty-seven, in accidental but dubious circumstances. Then in September 1978 the love of his life, John Scott, and Hugh MacDiarmid, his poetic father-figure, were buried within days of each other. These personal losses added to the stress of political turmoil, strikes, power cuts, war in the Middle East and economic inflation which shook Britain in the 1970s.

Yet his academic work had to go on, and his writing too. In some ways the 1970s provided a further breakthrough. Although *The Second Life* sold very well, its publishers could not promise a second volume. However, Morgan eventually found an internationally minded new publisher based in England. Michael Schmidt was director and editor of the small but enterprising Carcanet Press, and helped to shape the volume which established Morgan as a significant UK poet: *From Glasgow to Saturn* (1973). His creative editorial energies matched Morgan's poetic ones, and the mutual benefits of their partnership sustained both men through a troubled decade. In addition to *The New Divan* (1977), Schmidt also published two volumes of Morgan's translations and a collection of his academic essays during the 1970s, and commissioned his edited anthology, *Scottish Satirical Verse* (1980).

Morgan's work had already become better known after *The Second Life*, of course, so independent publishers now approached him with ideas. Thus the decade opened with several small-press productions, notably *Twelve Songs* (1970) and *Glasgow Sonnets* (1972) from Castlelaw Press, and *The Horseman's Word: A Sequence of Concrete Poems* (1970) and

The Whittrick: A Poem in Eight Dialogues 1955–1961 (1973)
from Akros Publications. Both of these were Scottish publishers. The *Songs* included such future favourites as 'The Apple's
Song' and 'The Loch Ness Monster's Song'.

Instamatic Poems (1972)

In 1972 a London bookseller, Ian McKelvie, asked Morgan for
a small collection for a new series of contemporary verse, and
was offered his new 'Instamatic' poems. Morgan described
them as being 'based on items reported in newspapers or
television and visualised by me as if someone had been present
and fixed the event with a camera'. This was part of his interest in new technology. The Instamatic camera used special
film to develop the image within minutes on the spot (rather
than having to finish a whole roll of film and then send it away
to be printed commercially). Morgan was always interested
in photography and film, and in new ways of thinking about
the mass media's impact on culture. As concrete poetry found
new meanings in layout and font, so the Instamatics explore
the impact of imagery, in the context of the most widely
consumed medium at this time: popular journalism of the
daily news.

They are also part of his exploration of time, with particular
moments caught in a flash. The poems were all headed by the
place, month and year in which the image was supposedly
captured, mainly events from 1971 with some from 1972. The
fifty-two poems were not in chronological order in the original
volume, but *New Selected Poems* presents a selection by date
order (pp. 49–56). However, the opening poem 'Glasgow 5
March 1971' ('With a ragged diamond / of shattered plate-glass
[...]') is first in both collections. The impassive observation of
a violent scene seems to mirror the two villains' faces that
'show no expression'. What they have done, however, is shock-
ingly detailed in the spurting of 'arterial blood', the face
'bristling with fragments of glass' and the arms 'starfished
out'. There is a contrast of couples too: the young couple (possibly window-shopping for a ring?), the two robbers, and finally
a pair of drivers passing by, unwilling to get involved. Morgan's
normal emotional and human involvement in Glasgow scenes

and people also seems to be absent, and this makes the poem all the more disturbing. Is an unspoken question being raised here about whether modern news media's dwelling on scenes of violence corrupts our ability to react with empathy? Like worldwide news coverage, the Instamatics range from Nice, Chicago, Nigeria, Burma, Vienna, Manchester, Bradford and Brazil to the mid-Atlantic and translunar space.

Morgan's selection of eleven Instamatics for *New Selected Poems* includes several on artists (Picasso, Pound, Stravinsky) and a multilingual Hungarian doctor-poet, as well as a teacher of Highland pipe music and North African Sufi dancers. He places these artists against rather desolate backgrounds, as if suggesting that the creative life demands a hard determination, putting one's art before family or friendships. Even the ancient Scottish art of the pibroch (bagpipe variations on a theme) is found in a difficult place. In 'Glasgow November 1971', the cherished 'speckled pipe' of the MacCrimmons is being played by the kilted young director of the College of Piping in a backcourt setting of speckled tenement walls 'against a speckled homely jungle / of glasses, thistles, dandelions, [...] Capstan packets and Lanliq empties'. The ancient culture of tartan and pipes blends like camouflage into its background of urban decay, and the camera records both.

These Instamatic poems certainly make a speckled collection, where amusing stories of human interest (or animal interest, in the cats' milk-lapping competition in a Glasgow pub) are set against grotesque scenes, as when a despairing precision-instrument mechanic from Darmstadt kills himself with a home-made guillotine. These are all true, we must remind ourselves. If we missed them in the newspaper, then seeing them now should be convincing (so long as we remember that we are seeing them in the mind's eye through the lens of an imaginary camera). Perhaps the most haunting poem of the sequence is 'Andes Mountains December 1972'. This presents a parody of religious Communion, as the surviving members of a Uruguayan rugby team whose plane crashed in the high Andes stay alive by eating the bodies of dead teammates, preserved in the snow. The team's name was the Old Christians.

Perhaps it is this combination of factual clarity and weird-
ness that soon appealed to young readers. It may also be that
Morgan's deliberate avoidance of emotion in this sequence
was a way of coping with his mother's death. She was a strong
character, who had taught her son not to show his feelings.
Other families might burst into tears, but the Morgans and
Arnotts were supposed to move ahead with life, no matter
what. Of course, it is dangerous to generalise from any one
mood of such a many-minded poet. His collection *From Glasgow
to Saturn*, published in 1973 and containing poems written
around this time, shows a great variety of tone. All the same,
a glance at the online listing of his poems held in the Department of Special Collections of Glasgow University Library
does reveal much translation activity in the months immediately after his mother's death, and then the Instamatic Poems.
These are interspersed with such poems as 'Death in Duke
Street' (p. 76), and 'Glasgow Sonnets' (pp. 82–86). These sonnets
explore the negative aspects of an urban renewal that Morgan
had found stimulating in the 1960s. There is also 'The Fifth
Gospel', which challenges the biblical Jesus with an even more
radical agenda: 'Give nothing to Caesar, for nothing is Caesar's.
[...] My yoke is not easy, and my burden is not light' (*Collected
Poems*, pp. 259–60). This may remind us of the challenge to
conventional Christianity in 'Message Clear', written when
his father was on the point of death.

From Glasgow to Saturn (1973)
Morgan had sent Michael Schmidt a large bundle of poems.
From these, Schmidt identified key themes, cut some poems
with less impact, and re-ordered the rest in a thematic order.
The collection begins with lighter, clear and energetic pieces
like 'Columba's Song', 'In Glasgow' and 'Floating off to Timor'
(pp. 57–59), which establish the Scottish city setting – exotic
travel is a nice fantasy, but reality beckons in the end:

We take in
the dream, a cloth from the line
the trains fling sparks on
in our city. We're better awake.

The love poems become more concerned with parting. In fact, Morgan's relationship with John Scott was deep but not exclusive, both men becoming involved with others from time to time. The love poetry in this collection is certainly more overcast than in *The Second Life*. In 'At the Television Set', for example, the poet considers the blue and yellow shadows thrown on the viewers' arms and faces, aware of time passing and the workings of time. At a cosmic level in space-time, action is preserved infinitely: 'For even in this room we are moving out through stars / and forms that never let us back' (p. 61). On earth, in a relationship that may be transient, he wonders what would last 'like a rock through cancer and white hair?' and finds no clear answer beyond their present moment together, when time too seems as if it might fall asleep.

The sense of the decay or destruction of love is caught in the three-part 'For Bonfires' (p. 62), nicely linked with Glasgow's slum clearance in the central description of 'the happy demolition men' heaping old door frames and rafters, shelves, toys, anything flammable, onto a pyre: 'And they all stand round / and cheer the tenement to smoke'. But their male energy in this second section of the poem is framed in the first by 'the gardener drifting / ghostly' as he gathers autumn leaves for burning; and in the final section by someone burning letters in a bucket. Aflame, the sheets seem to come alive: 'They put out claws and scrape the iron / like a living thing' – but soon subside. The person burning these personal letters (as Morgan burned many of his own before leaving for war service) seems to shrug off the loss of them, or at least hides the emotion with a sharp intake of breath:

> Let them grow cold
> and when they're dead
> quickly draw breath.

'Hyena' and other animal poems

More playful and exotic poems then shift the mood. Or perhaps they only appear playful. 'The Loch Ness Monster's Song' (p. 66) uses onomatopoeia and other sound effects to convey a clear impression of the monster rising out of the water to

play on the surface, before noticing tourists or monster-
watchers on the bank. The mood turns grimmer and decidedly
gruffer (using lots of those 'gr' sound-clusters associated with
unhappy noises, as in 'groan', 'gripe' or 'grizzle'). These 'folk'
seem to annoy the monster so much that it sounds as if it
might be swearing at them. The monster's intonation, by turns
perplexed and angry, is suggested by question and exclama-
tion marks. It then sinks under the water in a slow release of
bubbles: 'blm plm, / blm plm, / blm plm, / blp'. Again we are
drawn to the precision of the punctuation, with commas control-
ling the slow pace of submerging. So this 'nonsense poem'
makes a fair bit of sense. It has even been suggested that if
you turn the poem on its edge, the differing lengths of the
lines suggests the curving silhouette of the creature as it moves
across the loch. Whether or not this is true, there is much to
admire in the subtle way the poem is organised.

'Hyena' (p. 65) uses the immediacy of first-person narration
to convey this animal's character and threat. Its opening
remark 'I am waiting for you' is pointedly followed by an
explanation of how hungry and thirsty it is. The present tense
seems to draw us deeper into this dangerous encounter, as
our attention is drawn to its eyes, 'screwed to slits against the
sun'. So when it says at the end of the first stanza: 'you must
believe I am prepared to spring', we do believe!

There is arrogance in this creature, three times comparing
itself to the continent of Africa with regard to its coat and
craftiness and energy. This energy is itemised in its tireless
prowling movements: 'I trot, I lope, I slaver, I am a ranger'.
It calmly tells us 'I eat the dead', and the simple monosyllables
of this brief mission statement make it all the more horrifying.
Even when in the following stanza the hyena becomes almost
lyrical as it describes itself singing to the moon, the details of
its cold nocturnal habitat, 'mud walls and the ruined places'
and 'a broken drum', all suggest decay. Its question, 'Would
you meet me there in the waste places?' is a rhetorical one,
not a kindly invitation.

The reader is brought closer in towards the detail of the
hyena's murderous head: its muzzle, fangs and lolling tongue
– all the implements that help it make a 'golden supper' of a

lion's carcass. Even its supposedly laughing face becomes a threat: '[...] and I am laughing? / I am not laughing'. Instead it is waiting (and that is threatening too) for signs of weakness and impending death. Those signs involve elements that humans share with other mammals in the hyena's normal diet: 'foot', 'heart', 'sinews', 'eye', 'blood'. The hyena makes no distinction between our bones and those of other creatures. Seeing our humanity stripped away by such an alien understanding of the purpose of life may be the most frightening thing of all:

> My place is to pick you clean
> and leave your bones to the wind.

Morgan liked the independence of animals, particularly those such as wolves or midges that make human beings take notice. For example, 'The Third Day of the Wolf' (*Collected Poems*, p. 151) describes a lone Canadian timber wolf on the run, having escaped from a zoo. Thirty years later he would return to that theme in *Virtual and Other Realities* (1997) in a series of poems called *Beasts of Scotland* (written for jazz accompaniment). These include such typically Scottish animals as the red deer, golden eagle and midge, but also 'Wolf' (*Virtual and Other Realities*, p. 23), making the case for wolves to be released again in the Cairngorms:

> A little wildness please,
> a little howling to be heard from the chalets,
> a circling of yellow eyes at Aviemore.

We might sense that this desire for animals to move freely ran deep in his character, and was related to his own early experience of being hemmed in by social habits and judgments that he had to comply with – as a socialist poet in a conservative family, as a lecturer whose creative life was largely kept separate from his workaday teaching, and as a gay person whose sexuality could be expressed only by risking prosecution and disgrace. One poem that could move him deeply in performance was 'Afterwards' (p. 67). It describes the aftermath of

an atomic attack in a Far Eastern country, focusing on the
human suffering as described by a youngster. He has gone
out exploring with his sister and they find the skeleton of a
boy beside a bombed-out temple. The bony fingers still clasp
a tiny bamboo box, out of which comes the faint noise of a pet
grasshopper 'alive yet and scraping the only signal it knew
from behind the bars of its cage [...]'. They set it free. Morgan
identified very deeply with that instinct to communicate, even
under constraint.

To Saturn

Contrasting with this feeling of being caged, space exploration
always set Morgan's imagination free with thoughts of the
future. Different languages would be needed to experience it.
'Thoughts of a Module' (p. 68) is expressed in a simple machine-
syntax that provides an oddly intimate view of the first moon
landing from the module's viewpoint:

> All rock are samples. Dust taken I think.
> Is bright my leg. In what sun yonder.
> An end I think. How my men go.
> The talks come down. The ladder I shake.
> To leave that bright. Space dark I see.

Such broken speech also conveys something of the time-lapse
involved for those who actually watched the event on television, as the poet did.

Language and power is the theme of 'The First Men on
Mercury' (p. 69), enacted in an attempted dialogue. The contrast
between the naively superior language of the earthmen, talking
to the Mercurian natives in simple terms as if they were children, and the barbaric noises issuing from them in response,
is gradually transposed into a mixed dialect, with the speakers
each adopting terms from their different language systems.
However, the Mercurians prove much more capable than the
spacemen in assimilating the foreign speech, possibly through
some advanced sort of thought-transference. Taking hold of
the language of men, they send the spacemen back to planet

Earth able to speak only primitive Mercurian, with a menacing reminder that nothing will ever be the same again.

'Spacepoem 3: Off Course' (p. 70) uses concrete-like techniques of spatial position and repetition, as the second part of the poem is visually set 'off course' by an indented layout. Again Morgan makes use of images from television footage of early spaceflights ('the cabin song', 'the smuggled mouth-organ', 'the turning continents', 'the golden lifeline', 'the crackling headphone'). Once something goes wrong with the flight, however, the modifiers for these noun phrases become transposed in a way that eerily conveys the impression of a journey gone out of control and now adrift forever:

>   the turning silence
>   the space crumb   the crackling beard
>   the orbit mouth-organ   the floating song

From Glasgow

The collection ends with a return to earth, or to the patch of ground that was 1970s Glasgow. There is firstly a coursing surrealistic poem in five parts, called 'Rider' (p. 73). It features horses and Glaswegian poets, both varied in shape and style, and there is throughout the sequence a manic sort of energy that matches Morgan's idea of the city at its full potential to surprise. Yet surprise can quickly shade into shock, as in the pathos of 'Death in Duke Street' (p. 76). Supported by a youth who finds himself awkwardly at the centre of attention, an old man is dying on the pavement. This is the opposite of the positive outward movement of astronauts:

>   his eyes are fixed on the sky,
>   already he is moving out
>   beyond everything belonging

The poem works by its contrast of the crowd who mill round, comment and try to help, and the individual isolated by age and death. The poet's observation of the detail of the scene, sympathetic though it is, leaves him individually isolated too within his chosen observer role.

It was a role that, in Morgan's case, caused him to tackle moral issues in a determined way. 'Stobhill' (p. 77) deals with abortion, taking one case-history and allowing all those involved in the event to speak: the doctor, the mother, the father, the porter who carried the aborted baby down from the operating theatre to be incinerated, and the boilerman who heard whimpering sounds coming from the disposal bag. The baby's cry may remind us of the grasshopper scraping from inside its bamboo cage. Morgan's approach is not simplistic, since the multiple viewpoints reveal differing attitudes and values. He was, however, firmly on the side of living things, and the doctor and the porter in particular are condemned by their own poor excuses. The moral side of his poetry is clearly expressed. Michael Schmidt his publisher had persuaded him to include 'Stobhill' in the original *Selected Poems* of 1985, as he thought that schools would use it to raise discussion of difficult issues. In fact, in the 1990s Glasgow's *Daily Record* ran a feature against its use in Scottish schools. Perhaps this is what made Morgan retain it in *New Selected Poems* at the end of that decade.

From Glasgow to Saturn closes with a strong sequence of ten 'Glasgow Sonnets' (pp. 82–86). The choice of the sonnet form to deal with social issues is unusual, but not unique. Morgan had translated many Renaissance love sonnets from French, and had developed great skill in this strictly rhymed form. The discipline offered a challenge to his ingenuity, but the form also helps him here to focus the emotion that he felt at the stalled regeneration of his city, and indeed at the lives of its people still blighted by unemployment and poverty. Thus there is a sense of impassioned speech, all the more powerful for being contained within the fourteen lines permitted. If he had an English model for these socially minded sonnets, it was possibly John Milton's 'occasional' sonnets on persons and events. Morgan had also recently translated the sonnets on Venice of the German poet August von Platen (1796–1835). But the use of the sonnet form to analyse the detail of urban decay, the decline of heavy industry and the impact of government industrial policies on Clydeside shipbuilding in particular, was new and timely. As if to stress their wider political meaning, Morgan sent them to England for publication in *Stand* literary journal in Newcastle and the *Times Literary Supplement* in London.

It is interesting, as an example, to see how he builds the argument of the final tenth sonnet (p. 86) through a series of contrasts. These include the play on height and depth – from the thirtieth floor of the Red Road flats (eight multi-storey blocks in the north of Glasgow, designed to house 4,700 people) down to the pavement-level closemouth of 'single-end' flats (that is, one room functioning as kitchen, living- and bedroom). The 'Red' Road contrasts with 'high-rise blues' when the lifts break down. The skyward stretch of these flats prompts the ironic thought that, if most blocks of flats are sonnet-size (about fourteen floors), then these ones must have been stretched out to an ode.

This literary reference is part of raising a wider question about the use of a literary education. The poem has just focused on a schoolboy in one of the flats studying the tragedy of *King Lear,* and able to well imagine the scenes set by Dover cliffs because he himself lives on one. His life, which may offer a different future through education, is the opposite of the one facing those who remain in the slum conditions of single-ends 'that use their spirit to the bone'. When they trudge to the launderette, it is not only a load of washing that they carry: 'their steady shoes / carry a world that weighs us like a judge'. It is clear that in this final poem the poet puts himself and his readers to the test. What are we doing beyond writing and reading to make the world a better place for all?

From Glasgow to Saturn sold 1,700 copies in its first four months (extremely high sales figures for a poetry collection) and had to be reprinted several times. Probably the variety of stance, subject matter and form made the impact. No-one else in the UK then was writing with such verve across a comparable range of styles. Morgan's choice of twenty-one poems from this collection for *New Selected Poems* (out of fifty-two originally published) follows the original running order closely, but of course misses out some excellent work. The collection showed interesting developments of his concrete and sound poetry. Communication fractures in each of the final lines of 'Interferences: a sequence of nine poems' (*Collected Poems*, p. 253). 'The Computer's First Dialect Poems' and 'The Computer's First Code Poem' play with the language of machines (*Collected Poems*, pp. 276–77), and 'Itinerary' (p. 71) is a jokey performance piece made of Scottish sounds and scenery. The mood of the collection is also lightened by the comic potential of misunderstood long-distance telephone conversation in 'Boxers', and of relationship breakdowns in 'Letters of Mr Lonelyhearts' (*Collected Poems*, p. 271). 'The Gourds' and 'Last Message' (*Collected Poems*, pp. 261–62) take his science-fiction poetry further, as does the polemical energy of 'The Fifth Gospel' (*Collected Poems*, p. 259) for Morgan's self-positioning with regard to Christianity. His 1970s readers must have wondered where this restless talent would go next.

The New Divan (1977)

Uncharacteristically, Morgan went backwards, returning to his war experience in the Middle East. Those years had been a time of new experiences and growing up, but he had not been able to write about it then, nor in the thirty intervening years. He had retained very sharp sensory images of that period, however. Now, affected by news footage of the Arab–Israeli War of October 1973, he began to have nightmares of flashback intensity. Over a single week between 28 December 1973 and 3 January 1974, he wrote twenty poems. These would become the opening movement of his hundred-stanza war poem, 'The New Divan'. Sections of this poem were sent to different poetry magazines while he was still in the process of finishing it. It was published complete for the first time along with other poems in his Carcanet collection of the same title in 1977. The poem's title is an odd one, as 'divan' is an Arabic word which can mean three things: either a council of state, or a couch or bed, or a collection of poems. All three meanings are present within the one hundred stanzas, but this could be a source of confusion. The work as a whole never received as much discussion or praise as Morgan expected, and he came to think that it should really have been published as a separate volume.

Part of the problem was its Arabic form, for he uses the deliberately varied poetic format of the Middle-Eastern 'divan'. In the Arabic tradition, this lacks the usual narrative or chronological structure that underpins long poems in the Western tradition. It favours instead a deliberate variety of images and moods, from which listeners can select those parts that best suit a mood or occasion. British readers naturally found it hard to get a grip on what was really going on in the poem, at least until it reaches the final powerful stanzas of Morgan's own war experience as a medical orderly. It is possible to read the poem as a cinematographic form of composition, with vividly realised and intercut scenes and personalities, and several storylines intersecting past and present. Some of the incidents happen in archaeological time, at the site of an excavation in the desert. Others are city-based, in bedrooms or bazaars. Some stanzas include Morgan's fellow soldiers. Some involve mystical sages or Magi figures, able to observe the pettiness of human warfare and passions. He liked to think of the poems or storylines 'in divan', in discussion with each other as if at a council. Although it lacks any unifying narrative journey, the poem ends with 'paradise in prospect', and there are earlier elements which suggest a psychological progress through difficulties towards a realisation of the power of love, which is faithful yet unrequited.

The poem was too long to be included in *New Selected Poems*. Another longish poem opens the selection from *The New Divan*. 'Memories of Earth' (pp. 87–98) is a science-fiction voyage by beings from another universe, who travel down into a stone from which transmitted messages have been registered. Inside the stone is our universe, and inside that our world, and inside that the memories that come to haunt the explorers. It is perhaps a combined development of the earlier 'From the Domain of Arnheim' and 'In Sobieski's Shield'. The explorers are scientists whose role is to record observations in a dispassionate manner and then report back to the Council. Instead they find their personalities changed by this encounter with the earth and its inhabitants. They learn to disobey the Council, to ask questions, to conceal findings.

Some of their memories of earth are particularly haunting, for example the torture and execution of György Dózsa (1470–1514), a Hungarian man-at-arms who led a peasants' revolt against the nobility. There is also a vision of a man on a mountaintop who must be the Romantic poet William Wordsworth, who often composed his poetry aloud when out walking, with his dog alongside him ready to bark a warning when anyone approached. Here the poet is heard proclaiming verses from his autobiographical *The Prelude*: 'The emblem of a mind that feeds upon / infinity, that broods over the dark abyss [...]' (p. 91). The explorers also see a drive-in cinema and a concentration-camp gas chamber. Exploring the planet, however, they gradually come to experience, for the first time it seems, fragility, beauty and heroism. The last named quality resides in South Sea islanders, crossing the immensity of ocean in a canoe, and 'singing as they row'. Changed forever by their pity and admiration for the inhabitants of earth, the explorers have by the close of the poem assumed a 'human' ability to dissemble, hiding from the Council their efforts to match those taped visual memories to spore samples brought back from the earth:

> [...] handing to our memories of earth
> a life we'll make a source of life, begun
> in purposes of rebuked pain and joy.

Such working out of the meaning of mysterious messages is continued in a different mode in 'Shaker Shaken' (p. 101). The poem starts from the opening verse of an American Shaker poem of 1847, in which one discernible word appears among the meaningless syllables of glossolalia: 'love'. Through the following four stanzas more separate words emerge as Morgan gradually unfolds a magical vision of a tiger. What is clear is that this poet is determined to keep us, and himself, positive about human inventiveness. This includes what can be created by theatre and film directors and by politicians, as when 'On John MacLean' praises that early twentieth-century Scottish radical socialist (*Collected Poems*, p. 350).

Yet possibly the strongest poem in the collection is 'The World' (p. 98), where Morgan has to work hard against a prevailing 1970s gloom to stay hopeful. He does this cleverly by using two negatives to make a positive:

> I don't think it's not going onward,
> though no-one said it was a greyhound.
> [...]
> I don't see the nothing some say anything
> that's not in order comes to be found.
> It may be nothing to be armour-plated.

It is a difficult and compressed poem, with phantasmagoric scenes and images. These range from domestic settings ('At last someone got pushed mildly / on to a breadknife') to cosmic ones (the sun 'projecting / a million-mile arm in skinny hydro-gen / to flutter it at our annals'). Among the uncertainties and imperfections of life, only one thing seems sure: 'The past is not our home'. From that follows a determination to move forward in a sort of freedom, while we are physically able to do so:

> I don't think it's not being perfect
> that brings the sorrows in, but being soon
> beyond the force not to be powerless.

Time is the unspoken enemy here, and *The New Divan* ends with thoughts of death. Love might overcome it, and in 'Resur-rections' (p. 103) the poet links the scattering of the ashes of Chou En-lai, a skilful Chinese Communist politician who had died in 1976 ('Unknown he blows / like seed, is seed [...]'), with Christ's rising, birdsong and the poet's own exhilaration at falling in love and being 'caught up in another life'.

The collection ends with a beautiful sequence of ten 'Unfin-ished Poems' (*Collected Poems*, pp. 373–80). These were written for his friend, the poet Veronica Forrest-Thomson who had recently died of an overdose. Each of the poems is 'unfinished' in a different way, just as her poetic life had been cut short. It is a moving device, which has the reader eager to complete each poem, almost willing it into fullness. And it is also a way of refusing to let death have the last word.

'Winter' and other endings
But death, of course, cannot be ignored. In September 1977
Morgan wrote 'A Good Year for Death' (*Collected Poems*,
p. 403), recalling famous writers and singers who had died
that year. The poem recalls the opera diva Maria Callas, rock
stars Elvis Presley and Marc Bolan, novelist Vladimir Nabokov
and poet Robert Lowell. Written in the medieval 'ubi sunt'
form (from the Latin, 'where are they?') each verse commemo-
rates the dead artist's special talent and ends with the refrain:
'Death has danced her/his tune away'. It is an ancient form,
dwelling sadly on the transitory nature of life and beauty. The
love affair referred to in 'Resurrections' mentioned above was
with a much younger man. Now approaching sixty years of
age, Morgan must have been acutely aware of the difference
in their ages, and that his own time on earth was shortening
like the autumn days.

'Winter' (p. 118) was written in early December 1977, and
strikes a dark note that is unusual for this poet. It plays with
the opening lines of 'Tithonus', a dramatic monologue by the
Victorian poet Alfred, Lord Tennyson (1809–1892). In Greek
mythology Tithonus was granted perpetual life, but not perpetual youth, by the dawn goddess Aurora, and in Tennyson's
poem he now longs for death. Tennyson's poem opens:

> The woods decay, the woods decay and fall,
> The vapours weep their burthen to the ground,
> Man comes and tills the field and lies beneath,
> And after many a summer dies the swan.

Morgan keeps that autumnal scene, but fast-forwards it to
winter:

> The year goes, the woods decay, and after,
> many a summer dies. The swan
> on Bingham's pond, a ghost, comes and goes.
> It goes, and ice appears [...].

He rings further punning changes on Tennyson's lines later,
as if questioning their worth, or perhaps just playing with

words and punctuation to put off tackling what is on his mind. But the starkest contrast with Tennyson lies in Morgan's urban setting – not man tilling the fields, but city fog that has come alive and 'drives monstrous down the dual carriageway'. His flat overlooked the dual carriageway of Great Western Road in Glasgow, with Bingham's Pond just beyond that. There is a marked change now from his 1960s portrayal of Bingham's Pond in 'The Second Life' as a symbol of civic and emotional renewal. In his present mood everything seems dangerous and fraught, with tension evoked in the 's' alliteration: 'one stark scene / cut by evening cries, by warring air. / The muffled hiss of blades escapes [...]'. He cannot find a shred of blue sky, but instead only his own uncertainty. The longest line of the poem evokes a reaching out for something positive: 'dearest blue's not there, though poets would find it'. The line stretches out hopelessly, and is then undercut by present reality: 'I find one stark scene'. It is as if he has lost his talent. A real poet would surely find some hopeful blue sky, but he instead finds that the pane of ice outstares the paper he is writing on: 'that grey dead pane / of ice that sees nothing and that nothing sees'. The twin negatives fail to make a positive in this case.

When Morgan came to choose a motto for his *Collected Poems*, he wrote: 'Beti zeru urdin zati bat dago: bila ezazu'. No translation is given, but it is a saying from the ancient Basque language: 'There is always one shred of blue in the sky: search for it'. If in the winter of 1977 he failed to find one fragment of blue, there must have been a reason, apart from growing older. The summer had been an unhappy one, with messy repairs to cracks in the walls of his flat, books piled everywhere and plaster dust coating everything. Worse, a holiday with John Scott in Tenerife had ended in a bitter quarrel, and they would not meet again before John died of cancer a year later. Morgan could never write poetry with anyone else in the house, even in a different room, and thus lived alone. The lives of the two men were so separate that, despite their deep affection and seeing each other almost every week, they often quarrelled when living and travelling in close proximity on holiday. But this time Morgan had remained distant and made no effort towards reconciliation. He would never forgive himself. 'Winter' finds him experiencing a cold separation before their final one.

Star Gate (1979)

Some of his grief would pour itself into *Star Gate: Science Fiction Poems* (1979). This set of fourteen poems explores both atomic inner space, as in the lively 'Particle Poems' (p. 104), and also outer space in the tenderness of 'A Home in Space' (p. 106). This builds beautifully in linked lines (the ending of one line being taken up as the opening of the next, extending it in a new direction) to the human needs of voyagers in 'space that needs time and time that needs life'. But life in space and time must also include death. The final sequence, 'The Moons of Jupiter', sets personal grief against the cosmos. The surface of the planet 'Io' (p. 110) might well be John Scott's industrial Lanarkshire (the miners are on strike after a fatal accident) but it is also like hell (these are sulphur mines). There has been a funeral, 'Empty though not perfunctory', and now the 'weird planetman's flute from friends in grief' rises into 'the raw thin cindery air' millions of miles from home. In the final poem 'Callisto' (p. 112) the lunar landscape has been scarred by meteorites into a 'slaty chaos' that still cannot prevent the ongoing human quest: 'our feet, our search, our songs'. Life must go on. Yet the pits and mounds on this planet remind the narrator

> of one grave long ago
> on earth, when a high Lanarkshire wind
> whipped out the tears men might be loath to show [...]

The narrator refers to the shame he felt by the graveside listening to the 'perfunctory' priest (that word is used again, as in 'Io', and certainly Morgan had little sympathy with John's Catholic funeral). His private thoughts dwelt on everything 'that left us parted on a quarrel'. He ends on a note of dignity and muted hope:

> These
> memories, and love, go with the planetman
> in duty and in hope from moon to moon.

5. TOWARDS A DIFFERENT SCOTLAND

Poems of the 1980s

Morgan's first Collected Poems was published in 1982: *Poems of Thirty Years*. It was dedicated to John Scott. It included thirty-six uncollected poems from 1976 to 1981, and twelve of these are in *New Selected Poems*. They show Morgan in various moods, from the comic exploiter of flawed meanings in sound in 'The Mummy' (p. 114) and print in 'Little Blue Blue' (p. 122: based on a misprinted title of 'Little Boy Blue' by Norman MacCaig), to the serious self-analysis of 'The Coals' (p. 121), reflecting on the self-reliance and discipline which he had learned from his mother, 'which is both good and bad':

> You get things done,
> you feel you keep the waste and darkness back
> by acts and acts and acts and acts and acts,
> bridling if someone tells you this is vain,
> learning at last in pain.

Within this mindset, he finds the hardest thing 'is to forgive yourself for things undone'.

The most remarkable poems of this section show Morgan using dramatic monologue and narrative forms to try on, as it were, various possible selves and voices: the dramatist Shakespeare, the monster Grendel, the storyteller Jack London, and the acrobat Paul Cinquevalli. Each of these men is an outsider. The dramatist exists beyond both stage and auditorium; the monster is shunned by men and inhabits the darkness; Jack London is portrayed as a dropout from Paradise; and Paul Cinquevalli is a marvel, extraordinary in his skills as a juggler, but shunned too in old age. It is not hard to see in each of these an element of the poet's personality being explored.

'Instructions to an Actor' (p. 116) speaks as Shakespeare, coaching a young boy actor in the difficult role of Hermione, the wronged queen in *The Winter's Tale*. She is thought to be dead but is not, and now must re-appear as a statue that very gradually comes to life, to offer her now grieving husband a

51

second chance. The focus here is on the steady work involved in artistry, for the boy must remain stock-still while eighty lines are spoken. But the poem also considers the confidence needed by both actor and writer. Shakespeare has no doubts about his own gifts ('O this is where I hit them / right between the eyes, I've got them now – / I'm making the dead walk –'). But he depends upon and encourages the ability of a young actor to enact this crucial change of mood: 'and there's nothing / I can give you to say, boy / but you must show that you have forgiven him'. Morgan's recent reflections on his own character are hinted at by a reference to an earlier poem: 'Forgiveness, that's the thing. It's like a second life'. There may well be a reference even further back, to a similar theme of forgiveness in another of Shakespeare's late plays: *The Tempest*, Act V, Scene 1, line 195: '[...] I have / Received a second life [...]'.

There is a positive sense of the teaching relationship between the famous playwright and the unknown young actor, conveyed with warmth and encouragement: 'I know you can do it. – Right then, shall we try?' (p. 117). Morgan himself in the 1980s was increasingly a mentor to younger Scottish poets. He would also become much more involved in theatrical work, with adaptations of *The Apple Tree: a medieval Dutch play* (1982) and *Master Peter Pathelin*, translated from French (1983) for a group called The Medieval Players, besides the libretto for Kenneth Leighton's opera *Columba* (1981). His work in drama would be extended in the 1990s.

'Grendel' (p. 123) is the fen-dwelling monster from the Old English epic *Beowulf*, which Morgan had translated on his return from war service. His attraction to the language was partly also to the sense of isolation that its poetry could express (as in 'The Seafarer' and 'The Wanderer' which he translated). This paralleled his troubled situation as a gay man at that time. As mentioned earlier, it was not until 1980 that Scottish laws against homosexuality were repealed to bring them into line with 1967 changes in England and Wales. Possibly this recent change reminded Morgan of the outsider life he had lived for sixty years. Grendel is portrayed as the watcher at the feast in the drinking hall, gazing in at the physicality and warlike energies of male life in a warrior society. 'Who would be a man?' Grendel wonders. 'Who would be the winter sparrow / that flies at night by mistake into a lighted hall / and flutters the length of it in zigzag panic' before finding its way out to safety in the dark? The analogy of the sparrow's flight for man's short life, coming from darkness and disappearing into it after a brief time in the light, comes from the Old English monk and historian, the Venerable Bede. The power of the poem comes from the tension of attraction and repulsion that Grendel feels for ordinary men and their 'hideous clamorous brilliance'.

'Jack London in Heaven' (p. 124) presents another alter ego. Jack London (1876–1916) was an adventurer, sailor, prospector, largely self-educated socialist reporter and gifted storyteller. The poem sets him in heaven, arguing with the archangels against the regime of prayers and worship. He is 'a spoilt angel', forever gazing down through the clouds at the waters of San Francisco Bay where he sailed, drank and fished with his friends in the early days. He would write his fictions out of that rough male world. He crammed to get into university, but having succeeded 'took a boat out on the ebb / to be alone where no book ever was'. So in heaven he pines for earth: 'they cannot make me a heaven / like the tide-race and the tiller / and a broken-nailed hand [...]'. The poem evokes not merely Morgan's long quarrel with traditional religion, but his love of voyages, freedom and the sea. He was happy to discover that the Latin name of the British heretic Pelagius (c. 360–c. 420), who denied the doctrine of original sin and defended innate human goodness and free will, was a translation of his native name 'Morgan', and that it signified a wanderer on the open sea.

'Cinquevalli' (p. 127) is a wonderful poem on the transience of fame, but also on the true source of the seemingly superhuman skills of a gifted and determined artist. It quickly became identified with its creator. Morgan was intrigued when he came across an old postcard image of this Victorian acrobat and juggler, famous in the music halls in his day and yet almost forgotten a mere sixty years after his death in 1918. It was the 'bundle of enigmas' that attracted poet to performer: 'Half faun, half military man; almond eyes, curly hair, / conventional moustache [...] half reluctant, half truculent, / half handsome, half absurd [...]'. The poem recounts how Cinquevalli took up juggling while recovering from a fall from the trapeze. Out of adversity and mischance he discovers an even greater skill in juggling through practice and dexterity. Morgan's nimbleness with words matches and catches the juggler's astonishing tricks.

The poem works as a parable of poetry too. The trick of balancing billiard balls one on top of the other only works because 'the spheres are absolutely true. / There is no deception in him. He is true.' Virtuosity, whether gymnastic or poetic, cannot be faked. It was only by honest ceaseless work of writing and imagination that Morgan could fulfil the potential of his creative intelligence. Yet this poem is also a narrative of the pathos of time passing, and of the rejection that may come with age. Cinquevalli's Brixton neighbours hound him as a German spy during the First World War, because of his Polish name. Shortly before the Armistice this man 'of balance, of strength, of delights and marvels' is lowered 'in his unsteady box at last into the earth'.

Sonnets from Scotland (1984)
In trying out such new 'identities' as dramatist, outsider, rebel and entertainer, Morgan was possibly taking stock of his talents for the 1980s. Newly retired from university teaching, and having been finally separated from someone who had represented some kind of emotional security, he was ready to devote his energies more fully to Scotland's cultural and political life. A final bitter event of the unhappy 1970s had been the failure of the Scottish people to vote in sufficient numbers for devolution of political power from London to a Scottish Assembly.

Sonnets from Scotland (Mariscat Press, 1984) was written partly in response to this political let-down. Morgan felt it was important not to be pessimistic over the result, but to see it instead as a spur to writers whose work could help to create a more confident sense of Scottish identity. In the 1980s, Glaswegian writers Alasdair Gray, James Kelman, Tom Leonard and Liz Lochhead all published important work, and the Sonnets were part of that creative climate. He began the series in 1982, and the first sonnet written was 'The Solway Canal' (p. 149) which imagines a future journey by hydrofoil along an imagined canal dividing Scotland from England. This perhaps reveals the political impetus behind the series.

In the end, there were fifty-one sonnets, plus an additional one for the back cover, in praise of a 'Mariscat'. It is dedicated to Hamish Whyte, a Glasgow librarian who had become Morgan's bibliographer as well as his Scottish publisher through his Mariscat Press. The epigraph also points up the political intention. It is from the original German of *The Caucasian Chalk Circle* (1954) by the Communist dramatist Bertolt Brecht: 'O Wechsel der Zeiten! Du Hoffnung des Volks!' ('O times that change and bring hope to the people!'). So there was hope for Scotland yet, but only if the perspectives of time were borne in mind. This meant that past, present and future Scotlands, together with the inhabitants of this changing place, must become familiar again through imagination and learning. The epigraph is not translated. The poet may be suggesting that Scots should find out about their world, and about world literature and other political systems, in order to move forward with real confidence and independence of spirit.

'Slate' and other sonnets

Why begin the series with 'Slate' (p. 130)? The poem begins with a paradox, claiming that: 'There is no beginning'. So the poet is pointing not only to the unknown vastness of space-time in which Scotland stands, but also perhaps to this country's paradoxical nature, which is ancient in geological terms, and also fairly old in political terms (a hard-won nationhood was attained in the Wars of Independence seven centuries ago), but which relatively recently, with the Act of Union of 1707, had become part of a larger 'united' kingdom. Part of the point of this sequence will be to explore other versions of Scotland's story, with characters rarely mentioned in the standard histories. There will be imagined trajectories, too, of potential future Scotlands floating free of the short time-span of history that we know.

There are also the important layers of meaning in the title – of 'a clean slate' (to start afresh, with a blank space on which

new messages may be written) and 'put it on the slate' (keep
a record of our debts). Thus the sonnets will offer fresh ways
of looking at Scotland, and also ways of remembering what
we owe to past individuals who stayed here. In choosing to
place this poem first, Morgan is probably also remembering
how he learned to write as a child, with a slate pencil on a
piece of slate. As he would later describe it on programme
notes for a community drama devised by the Working Party
theatre group in 2004: 'It was a revelation / When words
appeared / Writing on a piece of earth / With another piece of
earth [...]'. *Sonnets from Scotland* will describe the variety
and potential of 'a piece of earth' that Scots call home.

Who are the 'we' who in this sonnet saw Lewis and Staffa
being formed, who watched as 'Drumlins blue as / bruises were
grated off like nutmegs [...]'? These intelligent presences are
able to appreciate colour and other sensory detail ('blue as
bruises' brings a close tactile sense) while also being above
time, able to watch millennia passing, and 'tens / of thousands
of rains, blizzards, sea-poundings [...]'. They are time-travellers
whose recorded images create the poem. They provide a remarkable commentary on the processes of erosion and geological
change that will in time produce not only slate, through meta-
morphosis of clay, but also human beings and their memories.
But 'That was to come'. At the start of the series we are in
a world of stone, with its 'empty hunger'. Perhaps this hard
world of 'flint, chalk, slate' is hungering for human habitation.
We are being invited to read on through pre-history into ancient
history and myth and then onwards into the present day and
beyond, in order to see what Scotland has to offer. As in the
earlier poem 'At the Television Set' (p. 61), every event that
happens seems to remain potentially present in time, encoded
there and ultimately accessible to intelligence.

Thus the *Sonnets* bring together some of Morgan's key
interests: science fiction, journeys through time and across
difficult terrain, Scotland and its history, nuclear warfare's
destructiveness, the work and lives of writers, philosophers
and scientists. We see him taking on the role of national poet,
the poet as teacher and as a source of national memory and
warning. All these people were in Scotland, he is saying: Seferis,

Lady Grange, Poe, De Quincy, Pontius Pilate, Tait, Hutton, Solovyov. You don't know who they are? Well, find out, and come to understand and value your country more securely in the process. Morgan's friends, students and colleagues are here too, in the dedicatory initials to some sonnets, marking a shared enthusiasm or project. Scotland's languages are heard: Pictish, Latin, French and (Glaswegian) Scots. The poet himself is caught in different moods. In 'After a Death' (p. 143) he is at his table writing, in a mood of self-criticism observed by the time-travellers: 'selfish, ruthless, he / uses people, floats in an obscure sea / of passions [...]'. He is redeemed to some extent by his experience of 'what is eternally due / to love that lies in earth in cold Carluke'. In 'The Poet in the City' (p. 144) the travellers pause and find him 'solitary but cheerful in / Anniesland, with the cheerfulness you'd win, / we imagined, through schiltrons of banked fears'.

A 'schiltron' is a spear-formation. Its use on the battlefield by Bruce and Wallace reaches back through the Wars of Independence to Viking, Anglo-Saxon and Pictish military practice. Modern military practice and its aftermath appear in 'The Target', 'After Fallout' and 'Computer Error: Neutron Strike' (pp. 146–47). A horn refrain is gradually heard in several sonnets. Is it a battle horn? In the last line of the final sonnet, 'The Summons', its purpose is revealed: 'A far horn grew to break that people's sleep' (p. 151).

By this point, the travellers are reluctant to go. Like the explorers in the earlier 'Memories of Earth', they have become unaccountably fond of the place and its people: Scotland is 'like a slate we could not clean / of characters, yet could not read, or write / our answers on [...]'. So the slate of the opening poem has been inscribed by an affecting history, all the more involving because some of it is yet to come, and beyond the experience even of these far travellers. The whole sequence, indeed, possesses something of the mysterious attraction of this place. These space visitors feel it, and so did those who first read the sequence in the 1980s. As the novelist and poet James Robertson recalled, in *From Saturn to Glasgow* (2008), a collection of fifty favourite poems by Morgan, *Sonnets from Scotland* was:

a hugely uplifting read during a politically frustrating time. Morgan seemed to reinvent Scotland's past, present and future. In 'The Coin' space travellers find a coin, a relic from a country that once existed – Scotland, but not a Scotland that has ever yet been. The poem asks if this is a Scotland we can attain? How long will it last? But there is great optimism in the last lines which still fills me with hope and pleasure whenever I read them.

One side of the coin is stamped *One Pound* and the other side *Respublica Scotorum*, the Scots Republic. Every reader will find favourites to return to: 'Pilate at Fortingall', 'Theory of the Earth', 'The Coin', 'The Solway Canal', 'On Jupiter' and 'A Golden Age' come to mind. So the mysterious attraction felt by the space travellers also extends to the life of the collection in the minds of many readers. What is also mysterious is the skill with which Morgan rhymes so cleverly and dexterously that the sonnets unfold with a lively naturalness that belies their art.

From the Video Box (1986)
In real life, Morgan continued to be fascinated by changes in technology. Television, video and satellite broadcasting caught his attention. Channel 4 was established in 1982, and one of its innovations was the use of a 'video box' in major cities. These allowed viewers to make comments on programmes, and the footage was then edited for *Right to Reply*. Watching this programme was the inspiration for *From the Video Box* (1986), the next Mariscat Press production. As we have seen, Morgan was fond of writing poems in series, and Mariscat would publish limited editions of such work on a regular basis, often in pamphlet format. These would then be gathered up along with individual poems into book publications from Carcanet for the wider UK and international market. This meant that Morgan's work could appear more frequently from a local publisher for his Scottish audience, creating greater engagement with them than if there had been intervals of years between publications.

From the Video Box is a sequence of twenty-seven poems arranged in thematic groups of three. The poems present viewers' comments on programmes dealing with books, scratch video, colour TV, Shakespeare, *not* TV programmes, subliminal images or messages, special televisual or video developments, satellite TV, and favourite programmes. Of course, these comments are from 'viewers' of 'programmes', each one a product of the poet's entertaining imagination. Probably for reasons of space, only the last three poems in the sequence (on favourite poems) appear in *New Selected Poems*, but these include one admired by many poets, 'From the Video Box 25' (p. 152).

In this poem Morgan focuses on the winner of 'that strange world jigsaw final', supposedly televised. He is 'a stateless person [...] small, dark, nimble, self-contained', who is able, after days and nights of almost superhuman concentration, to complete a jigsaw of an aerial image of one featureless stretch of mid-Atlantic: 'to press that inhuman insolent remnant together'. That summary of the poem probably makes it seem the most boring TV programme imaginable, but Morgan's control of the pacing, tension and physical detail of the contest turns it into a vivid parable of the creative mind, as it slowly, patiently, with determination, stamina and huge force of intelligence pieces together a work of art from tiny details until it emerges, meaningful and complete. It probably appeals to poets because the poem is about the imagination – the ability to create pictures, not from nowhere but from fragments of experience, real or imagined, and from the unexpected and often pictorial comparisons that metaphors and similes make in the reader's mind.

Themes on a Variation (1988)

Morgan's next Carcanet collection was *Themes on a Variation* (1988), and it includes both the 'Sonnets from Scotland' and 'From the Video Box' poems, as well as a sequence of fifty 'Newspoems (1965–1971)'. These are cut from actual newsprint or advertisement headlines or text, manipulated to reveal hidden messages, often jokey. The dating places them in the period of his concrete poetry, and their presence some twenty years later shows Morgan's determination to reflect the variety not only of life but also of his responses to it. Most artists (he may be suggesting) can write variations on a theme, but he himself prefers to take variation as the key theme in itself. This approach offers the advantage of stimulation for his readers, perhaps, but also the disadvantage of leaving himself open to the criticism of a lack of depth – of going further instead of deeper into any one issue. As if to forestall the criticism, the opening poem in the collection is 'The Dowser' (p. 156), developed from an actual experience of dowsing for subterranean water in Ireland but here transposed to take in his experience of the North African desert in the 1940s. There is also the deeply 'politically incorrect' poem, 'Rules for Dwarf-Throwing' (p. 158), which is a funny satire on the kind of 'health and safety' rules that circumscribe many areas of modern life (its inspiration was an article in a Civil Service departmental magazine).

The last work chosen for *New Selected Poems* from this collection is 'Dear man, my love goes out in waves' (p. 157). It is the best-known of a set of poems on a moderately happy love affair. These are neatly rhymed but seem to lack the emotional intensity of his earlier love poetry. As he approached his seventieth birthday in 1990, he had decided to 'come out' in a public way as a gay man. This was belated, perhaps, but nevertheless daunting for someone who had had to live for so many years under threat of exposure and possible imprisonment. He was of his generation in this regard. The novelist and poet Christopher Whyte interviewed him, and this appeared as 'Power from things not declared' in *Nothing Not Giving Messages: Edwin Morgan, reflections on work and life*, edited by Hamish Whyte (Polygon, 1990). The book was a collection of interviews given by the poet, together with eighteen of his articles, statements or lectures on the practice of poetry and translation. With *About Edwin Morgan*, edited by Robert Crawford and Hamish Whyte (Edinburgh University Press, 1990) and a new *Collected Poems* from Carcanet Press, it was published to coincide with his birthday.

Approaching this birthday, Morgan was working on a collection of seventy poems on 'social themes'. These would appear in the new decade as *Hold Hands Among the Atoms* (1991). Scotland was a different place by the end of the 1980s. It had lived through the monetarist reforms of a Conservative government led by Margaret Thatcher, which reduced inflation and increased economic performance in the longer term, but resulted in increased unemployment, redundancies and friction with trade unions through privatisation of formerly nationalised industries. All of this worked against the generally more left-wing values of the Scottish electorate. In Morgan's case, his socialism was also challenged internationally by the collapse of Communism in Eastern Europe towards the end of the decade. Although he had never been as doctrinaire as Hugh MacDiarmid in his support of Communism, preferring to judge its impact on particular countries and contexts, he had travelled quite widely in Russia and in the Eastern European countries it had dominated since 1945, such as Hungary, Poland, Czechoslovakia, Yugoslavia, Romania and Albania. He was now shaken by the speed of the collapse of their various regimes, and perhaps even more so by the resurgence there of Orthodox Christianity or Catholicism which had been repressed for so long.

Since his own knowledge of these countries had come largely through his work as a translator and reviewer of their literatures from the 1950s onwards, it is probably time to consider his translations in broad outline. Who were these poets whom he spent hours and days translating, and why did they matter to him?

6. TRANSLATION: VARIATIONS ON THE THEME OF POETRY

Edwin Morgan was a prodigious translator. His 487-page *Collected Translations* (Carcanet Press, 1996) is only 100 pages lighter than his 595-page *Collected Poems* (re-published in paperback in the same year), and he certainly wanted both volumes to be considered as dual dimensions of his work as a poet. He is particularly known for his translations of Eastern European poetry, especially of Russian poets such as Boris Pasternak, Vladimir Mayakovsky and Andrei Voznesensky, and of Hungarian poets such as Sándor Weöres, Lajos Kassák and Attila József. His skill in translating from both those languages was recognised from the 1950s onwards by poets and editors in both countries, and by awards such as the Hungarian Grand Cross in 1997 for his services to the country's literature. His Spanish translations are less well-known, but stretch from fifteenth-century Spanish romances to Garcilaso de la Vega in the sixteenth century, and from the nineteenth-century Galician poet Rosalía de Castro to García Lorca, Luis Cernuda and Pablo Neruda in the twentieth. His 1960s Portugese translations of concrete poets from the Noigandres group in São Paulo, Brazil, include avant-garde work by Haroldo and Augusto de Campos and Edgard Braga. These names are by no means a complete list of even this relatively minor Hispanic section of his output. The index to *Collected Translations* features sixty-seven poets and many others remain uncollected. But they illustrate something of the breadth of Morgan's life-long engagement with poetry in other languages. He also worked from French, German, Italian, Latin, Greek and Old English.

French was the language he first translated, with versions of Paul Verlaine (1844–1896) in his upper school years. These coincided with his own first poems, and the habit of writing poems and translations in tandem became a life-long pattern. More accurately, he would often turn to translation when not caught up in his own poetry, or sometimes as a spur to poetry when shifting from teaching mode to writing mode at the start of university vacations, when most of his poetry was written.

Some functions of translation

Translation seems to have fulfilled various purposes in his creative and emotional life. These can be divided into general and more personal functions.

Generally, translation is an immediate way of enlarging a small country's literature, giving readers access to a far wider range of texts and styles than could be managed locally. Writers have been doing this in Scotland from the earliest times. The most famous example is probably the translation of the Roman epic poet Virgil's *Aeneid* by Bishop Gavin Douglas (c. 1474–1522). Completed around 1513, this medieval Scots translation of the classic text was the first to be published in the British Isles. One of the cultural advantages of this process is that translation is not simply borrowing other writers' content. Working to find the equivalent of linguistic or stylistic effects in the poem being translated often has the effect of making the poet extend his or her own language to meet the challenge of the foreign one.

Secondly, for Morgan translation meant involving Scotland in international and modern visions of reality and the arts. Just searching the internet for detail on the poets he translated can be an educational experience. Their names open up political, historical and cultural vistas, particularly on Eastern Europe. Cultural movements that in his view had been undervalued in Britain, and perhaps in Scotland in particular, can be explored through following the trail of translations – constructivist, surrealist, concrete or minimalist. They show artistic trends impacting on world cultures.

Thus his translations can be seen to exemplify Morgan's modernity. The use of multiple perspectives, references, fragments of knowledge from diverse times and places was a typical strategy used by modernist artists trying to express the speed and fragmentariness of modern culture. Modernism is a complex phenomenon, changing over the last decades of the nineteenth century and first half of the twentieth. But generally it is considered to be an artistic response to modern means of communication, both in print media such as newspapers and also in telegraphic and transport technology, as well as to changing scientific and philosophical views about humanity's

place in the universe, and about the nature of language itself.
This led to many experiments in form and style. Even listing
such features of modernism helps place Morgan's interests in
newspapers, machines, the city, language and formal experimentation among a broad group of fellow artists from many
countries. That he should want to translate their works for
himself is not so surprising. What is remarkable is that he
should do it so widely and so well.

Translation was helpful at a personal level too. His sense
of identification with the heroic austerity and isolation to be
found in Old English poetry has already been mentioned. In
his post-war isolation, he was particularly drawn to the poetry
of Maurice Scève (c. 1500–1564), a Renaissance poet who wrote
in the Petrarchan manner where the object of the poet's love
is distant or unobtainable. He also translated Petrarch, Tasso
and Marino at this time.

Translation was also a way of enriching Scots language.
Morgan was tremendously knowledgeable about Scots as a
poetic medium, taking forward MacDiarmid's experiments
with the language while retaining his own commitment to the
speech of real people that he could hear around him in Glasgow.
The fact that he translated both the German of Heinrich
Heine and the English of some of William Shakespeare's
Macbeth into the more literary 'synthetic' Scots advocated
by MacDiarmid, as well as the Italian of Michelangelo and
Leopardi, and the Russian of Solovyov and Blok, should not
take away from his commitment to modern Scots as it had
developed in urban industrial settings.

There were also some poets whom he came to translate out
of a deep sense of affinity, almost of identification. In fact, he
needed to feel some engagement with a foreign poet's attitudes
or artistry if he was to translate the work successfully. Some
poets were for him heroic figures in their commitment to both
poetry and their native lands. Vladimir Mayakovsky (1893–
1930) was one such hero, a remarkable poet and playwright,
a futurist and constructivist, who devoted his considerable
creative energies to carrying forward the social changes of the
Russian Revolution. The strain probably drove him to suicide,
and Morgan remembered reading a newspaper report about

this when he was ten years old. He tried first to translate this
avant-garde poetry into English but felt that this failed to
match the Russian's impact. Then he discovered that Scots
seemed to offer a racy inventiveness that captured more
of Mayakovsky's bravura performances. His translations,
published in *Sovpoems* (1961) and *Wi the Haill Voice* (1972),
made a significant impact.

Salvatore Quasimodo (1901–1968) was another poet he
admired. A Nobel Laureate and professor of literature in Milan,
he met Morgan when visiting Scotland in 1960, and liked his
translations. Morgan admired the Italian poet's development
from an early difficult symbolist style to his later poetry
showing deep concern for social issues and the fate of his
country. With Sándor Weöres (1913–1989) the admiration
was even greater. Morgan met him on a British Council trip
to Hungary in 1966, and discovered a writer of astonishing
technical ability in a wide range of styles, erudite and with
great linguistic virtuosity, yet still almost child-like in his
sense of humour. He was a poet of many voices, and Morgan
felt an immediate sense of kinship, translating many of his
poems. Working in Communist Hungary, Weöres had survived
disapproval and censorship from the Marxist regime.

There were other poets whose isolation or struggle against
fate affected Morgan emotionally. He responded to the rather
melancholy atmospheric details in the poetry of Eugenio
Montale (1896–1981), the play of light on water, crumbling
buildings, a face glancing in a mirror, the sound of an accordion
in the twilight. He recognised a similar loneliness in Giacomo
Leopardi (1798–1837). With the Hungarian poets Lajos Kassák
(1887–1967) and Attila József (1905–1937) the points of contact
were with their economic struggle, rugged individualism and
avant-garde attitude. Like Mayakovsky, József committed
suicide, and this sad sense of unfulfilled potential encouraged
his translator to strive to make him better known.

A theory of poetic translation

Morgan described how he worked in 'The Translation of Poetry'
(*Nothing Not Giving Messages*: p. 232–35) His approach
combined the idea of a 'flickering web' of pictorial, acoustic

and sensuous impressions that the translator picks up from early readings of the text. These provide a first sense of the foreign poem: its 'symmetry or ruggedness', line-length and rhyme, its 'close or open texture, curious or common vocabulary' – all taken in at a more or less impressionistic level, and stored at the back of the mind. At the next stage, the front of the mind focuses on a 'grid of meaning', derived from close work with dictionary and grammar, word by word and phrase by phrase, from beginning to end. Finally the translator re-focuses the grid of meaning on to the web of impressions: and 'when they coincide, the translator feels he can really see the poem'.

Then something curious happens as the actual translation begins. There is a search for equivalence across two languages, but not of the words of the foreign language so much as

> the words of *the poem itself*, which has attained some sort of non-verbal interlinguistic existence in the mind. [...] Without desiring to be mystical, I believe there does seem to be some sense [...] in which the poem exists independently of the language of its composition.

He then quotes from the critic Walter Benjamin: 'It is the task of the translator to release in his own language that pure language which is under the spell of another, to liberate the language imprisoned in a work in his recreation of that work'.

This view of the poem being translated as not 'belonging' to its original author would clearly be attractive to a youngish poet struggling to find his own direction, as Morgan was in the 1950s. There was affirmation in discovering oneself as a 'co-author' (at least) in the act of translating a poem. Morgan was also fond of Shelley's vision in *The Defence of Poetry* (1821, published in 1840) of the vast poem 'which all poets, like the co-operating thoughts of one great mind, have built up since the beginning of the world'. Whatever the truth of this view, his ability to identify with another poet's world, together with his accurate grip on formal elements such as rhyme and rhythm and his own inventive way with words, helped Morgan to become a remarkable translator long before his own break-through as a poet.

7. DRAMATIC POETRY AND POETIC DRAMA

In the 1990s Morgan would make more use of the media to communicate with a wider audience. *Hold Hands Among the Atoms* was published in 1991, but many of its seventy poems on social themes had already appeared in journals and Scottish newspapers. He was also more involved in theatrical and musical performance of his work and so became even better known. We might see this as part of his view that writers in Scotland should have a national role in commenting on their society.

Poems of the 1990s

Approaching the millennium, his poetry was concerned with the beginnings and endings of life, reward and punishment, willpower, striving and strife. Two of the most moving poems focus on what remains of us after death. In 'Aunt Myra (1901–1989)' (p. 165), a man is clearing the house of an old woman after her death and finds himself moved by an old-fashioned object: her dance cards. These had little pencils attached, used to write down the names of partners promised for one dance or another. The man does not know what to do with the cards, so light and yet so weighted with memories of 'tender evenings' from an almost vanished past. There is tenderness in the poem too, with its contrast of the man brought to a standstill while the cards in his hand dangle from their pencil cords, evoking the twirling of vanished dancers. Aunt Myra was Morgan's mother's sister.

In 'Fires' (p. 166), memories of his parents bring back thoughts of his childhood, as he sang along to songs from 'some thin wild old gramophone that carried / its passion across the Rutherglen street'. This music from a neighbour's house seemed to call him to a sunny country where he might be happy, even for a moment, and all his misery would be burned away. This burning blends oddly with his parents' ashes, reduced to almost nothing – 'The not quite nothing I praise it and I write it'. Their life persists in the elderly poet writing his lines for them.

Neither poem suggests a religious dimension, but Morgan's translation of *Altus Prosator* (*The Maker on High*) (*Collected*

Translations, pp. 389–93) cannot avoid this. Attributed to St Columba, it is a powerful abecedarian poem, with each stanza beginning with a letter of the alphabet in sequence, A–Z. His translation matches the drive of the original's late Latin, where complex internal rhymes and echoes convey the force of Columba's mission to convert the Picts to Christianity. It describes the Fall of Satan and his angels, with their punishment in Hell. Morgan's main interest was not the religious theme but the fact that this was the earliest Scottish poem in written form.

His preferred view of things is found in *Demon* (1999), which speaks mainly in a devil's voice. But the speaker is more of a dæmon than a demon, namely a spirit holding a place midway between man and the gods, a more-than-human power or intelligence. This dæmon visits and comments on places the poet had also visited, such as Albania and the Auschwitz concentration camp in Poland. Nearer home in Glasgow, in 'The Demon in Argyle Street', a young tough tries to give the Demon a kicking and then wishes he hadn't. The Demon's voice is by turns harsh, seductive, mocking, cruel and, above all, defiant. It reflects something of its maker's character at this late stage, determined to keep searching for the secret of life: 'I don't come unstuck, I don't give up. / I'll read the writing on the wall. You'll see.' These are the Demon's parting words.

The sequence appeared in *Cathures: New Poems 1997–2001* (2002, pp. 93–115), co-published by Carcanet and Mariscat presses. The 1990s Carcanet collections were *Sweeping Out the Dark* (1994), which included many new translations, and *Virtual and Other Realities* (1997), notable for 'Beasts of Scotland', the series on Scottish animals (wildcat, salmon, conger eel, etc.) written to be set to music by the saxophonist Tommy Smith.

Poetry on stage
Morgan performed 'Beasts of Scotland' with Tommy Smith and his band at the Glasgow Jazz Festival in 1996. Together they also developed and performed 'Planet Wave' (1997), the first part of which brings *New Selected Poems* to a close (pp. 168–79).

Loosely based on *A Short History of the World* (1922, 1946) by science-fiction writer and novelist H. G. Wells, it was written for voice, jazz band and synthesiser. The big theme is time itself, with the repeated image of a wave appearing at different eras or historical events on Earth. These stretch from 20 Billion BC ('In the Beginning') through the early Earth and the destruction of the dinosaurs, on past the Flood, the Pyramids etc. to 'Copernicus (1543 AD)', whose observations of planetary movements would revolutionise human understanding of astronomy.

But it was drama that brought the greatest change to Morgan's writing, as publications accompanied theatrical productions of his work. In *Edmond Rostand's Cyrano de Bergerac: A New Verse Translation* (1992), a famous love story with a gay subtext was remade in boisterous fashion in inventive Glaswegian speech. His *Christopher Marlowe's Dr Faustus: a new version* (1999) explored issues of willpower and scientific endeavour. His interests in French literature and in Scots as a dramatic medium moved from the comedy and pathos of *Cyrano* to the classical tragedy of *Jean Racine: Phaedra: a translation of Phèdre* (2000). In that same millennial year, Morgan's AD: *A Trilogy of Plays on the Life of Jesus Christ* continued his engagement with Middle Eastern culture and history, causing controversy among Church groups because of its unconventional portrayal of Jesus. In all these he worked closely with different drama companies in Glasgow and Edinburgh. The focus on spiritual ambition (whether in saint or devil) already noted in his poetry, and on aspects of free will, identity and the afterlife, were acted out now through character and conflict, music and theatrical design. At the same time, he was pushing at the boundaries of urban Scots language, and asserting by example what it was capable of achieving in different genres.

In October 1999 Morgan was made Poet Laureate for Glasgow, with a commission to produce a substantial poem or sequence about Glasgow. He was also diagnosed with cancer, but continued to work intently despite the effects of chemotherapy. In fact, the thought of time running out spurred him onwards to complete the various projects undertaken.

Poems in a new century

For the title of his major 2002 collection Morgan chose an old name for Glasgow, *Cathures*. It contains the results of his time as the city's Laureate. There is a memorable set of nine dramatic monologues by people who had lived in or visited Glasgow, in reality or imagination. These include Morgan's 'ancestor' Pelagius, and Merlin and Thennoch (the mother of Mungo, the city's patron saint) as well as the industrialist John Tennant, the religious reformer George Fox, the surgeon John Hunter, and others. There is a great sense of energy and commitment throughout the sequence, each voice capturing the drama of a life. 'Changing Glasgow' (*Cathures*, p. 31) then records the poet's response to the city's street-life. There are more house-based poems, as his life became more circumscribed by illness, but also poems from musical commissions and a set of 'Cathurian Lyrics' in a newly invented rhyming form (*Cathures*, pp. 81–89).

Morgan used this Cathurian stanza form again in 'Love and a Life', a sustained reflection on his personal relationships early and late in a long life, but also on the variety of kinds of human love, including mystical or spiritual attachment. This sequence became part of his last major collection, *A Book of Lives* (2007), along with his great poem 'For the Opening of the Scottish Parliament, 9 October 2004' (*A Book of Lives*, p. 9). The collection was shortlisted for the major T. S. Eliot Award and won the Scottish Arts Council Sundial Book of the Year Award.

By now wheelchair-bound, he had to travel by ambulance to collect this award at the Borders Book Festival in Melrose. But he was always able to travel freely in his imagination. *Tales from Baron Munchausen* (2007) are new versions of the tall stories of a Hanoverian soldier who served in the Russian army against the Turks in the eighteenth century. Full of verve, speed and the trajectories of weapons and flight, these fantastic tales explore the borderlines between story-telling, lies and madness. They were written for dramatic performance in a show that travelled through Scotland, so Morgan's imagination was carried beyond his nursing home by proxy.

He continued striving to be creative into his final years, although physically weaker. He had careful oversight of a final collection, *Dreams and Other Nightmares: New and Uncollected Poems* (2010). Published for his ninetieth birthday, it contains poems written within the last two years of his life, including the last poem he worked on, the translation of an Old English riddle for an international anthology, *The Word Exchange* (2011). The riddle's solution, appropriately enough, is creation.

Two national poets?

When Edwin Morgan became Scotland's Makar, the country already had a national poet in Robert Burns. As a critic, Morgan did not write much about Burns, although he liked his personality and poetry very much indeed. He admired the range of his gifts – as a storyteller, a social commentator, a songwriter and entertainer. Morgan had a similar flair. Both poets cared deeply about Scotland, its culture, history and politics. Both wrote of the great heroes of Scottish independence, Wallace and Bruce, and challenged current attitudes, holding Scotland to account against events in the international politics of their age. 'Lines for Wallace' and 'The Battle of Bannockburn' appear alongside challenging poems on 'The Twin Towers' and 'The War on the War on Terror' in Morgan's last major work (*A Book of Lives*, pp. 14, 16, 42, 104).

But it was the power of Burns's imagination that particularly appealed to Morgan, and the combination of realism and strangeness in his work. The ability to shift quickly and unaccountably from the social world to unearthly otherworlds was a quality that both poets shared. So different in length of life, intellectual and social background and personality, still they might have been brothers – the one extrovert and the other more of an introvert, yet both born with that true poetic gift of imagination allied to a penetrating intelligence. Quick-witted and determined, each was able to respond wholeheartedly to the dazzling talent he had been given. Their poems constantly recall us to the full potential of the mind and heart. Such broad humanity, opposing 'any narrow party version of the truth', is the shared and resonant note of a clarion call to Scotland, that echoes also through the wider world.

8. FURTHER READING

Selected Poetry Collections by Edwin Morgan
Collected Poems (Manchester: Carcanet Press, 1996)
Virtual and Other Realities (Manchester: Carcanet Press, 1997)
New Selected Poems (Manchester: Carcanet Press, 2000)
Cathures: New Poems 1997–2001 (Manchester: Carcanet Press and Mariscat Press, 2002)
Tales from Baron Munchausen (Glasgow: Mariscat Press, 2005)
A Book of Lives (Manchester: Carcanet Press, 2007)
Dreams and Other Nightmares (Edinburgh: Mariscat Press, 2010)

Selected Translations
Collected Translations (Manchester: Carcanet Press, 1996)
The Colonnade of Teeth: Modern Hungarian Poetry, ed. George Gömöri and George Szirtes (Newcastle upon Tyne: Bloodaxe Books, 1996). Foreword and many translations by Edwin Morgan.
Attila József: Sixty Poems (Glasgow: Mariscat Press, 2001)

Selected Drama
Edmond Rostand's Cyrano de Bergerac. A new verse translation by Edwin Morgan (Manchester: Carcanet Press, 1992)
Christopher Marlowe's Doctor Faustus in a new version by Edwin Morgan (Edinburgh: Canongate, 1999)
Jean Racine's Phaedra: a tragedy. Translated by Edwin Morgan ((Manchester: Carcanet Press, 2000)
AD: A Trilogy of Plays on the Life of Jesus Christ (Manchester: Carcanet Press, 2000)

Selected Critical Prose by Edwin Morgan
Essays (Cheadle Hulme: Carcanet New Press, 1974)
Crossing the Border: Essays on Scottish Literature (Manchester: Carcanet Press, 1990)
Nothing Not Giving Messages: Edwin Morgan: reflections on work and life, ed. Hamish Whyte (Edinburgh: Polygon, 1990)

'A Poet's Response to Burns' in *Burns Now*, ed. Kenneth
 Simpson (Edinburgh: Canongate Academic, 1994) pp. 1–12
'A Scottish Trawl' in *Gendering the Nation: Studies in Modern
 Scottish Literature*, ed. Christopher Whyte (Edinburgh:
 Edinburgh University Press, 1995) pp. 205–22

Biography

McGonigal, James, *Beyond the Last Dragon: A Life of Edwin
 Morgan* (Dingwall: Sandstone Press, 2012)

Resources for Schools

Cockburn, Ken, *The First Men on Mercury: A Poem by Edwin
 Morgan* Teaching ideas from the Scottish Poetry Library
 (Association for Scottish Literary Studies, 2009)
MacGillivray, Alan, *Aspects of Edwin Morgan* Teaching Notes,
 Autumn 2001 (Association for Scottish Literary Studies, 2001)
metaphrog, *The First Men on Mercury: A comic-strip adapta-
tion* (metaphrog and Association for Scottish Literary
 Studies, 2009)
Thomson, Geddes, *The Poetry of Edwin Morgan*, first edition:
 Scotnotes 2. (Association for Scottish Literary Studies, 1986)
Watson, Roderick, *17 Poems of Edwin Morgan: A Commentary,
 with Readings by Edwin Morgan* (CD: Association for Scot-
tish Literary Studies, 2004)
— *23 Poems of Edwin Morgan: A Commentary, with Readings
 by Edwin Morgan* (CD: Association for Scottish Literary
 Studies, 2005)

Selected Critical Studies on Edwin Morgan
and his context

Brown, Ian and Riach, Alan, eds, *The Edinburgh Companion
 to Twentieth-Century Scottish Literature* (Edinburgh: Edinburgh University Press, 2009)
Crawford, Robert and Whyte, Hamish, eds, *About Edwin
 Morgan* (Edinburgh: Edinburgh University Press, 1990)
Gifford, Douglas, Dunnigan, Sarah and MacGillivray, Alan,
 eds, *Scottish Literature in English and Scots* (Edinburgh:
 Edinburgh University Press, 2002) 'Scottish Poetry after
 1945: Edwin Morgan' pp. 771–75

McGuire, Matthew and Nicholson, Colin, eds, *Edinburgh
    Companion to Contemporary Scottish Poetry* (Edinburgh:
    Edinburgh University Press, 2009) 'Edwin Morgan'
    pp. 97–110
Nicholson, Colin, *Edwin Morgan: Inventions of Modernity*
    (Manchester: Manchester University Press, 2002)
Schmidt, Michael, *An Introduction to Fifty Modern British
    Poets* (London: Pan Books, 1979) 'Edwin Morgan'
    pp. 314–20
Watson, Roderick, *The Literature of Scotland: The Twentieth
    Century* (Basingstoke: Palgrave Macmillan, 1984, 2007)
    'New Visions of Old Scotland' pp. 203–15
— 'Internationalising Scottish Poetry' in *History of Scottish
    Literature, Volume 4: Twentieth Century* ed. Cairns Craig
    (Aberdeen: Aberdeen University Press, 1989) pp. 311–30
Whyte, Christopher, *Modern Scottish Poetry* (Edinburgh: Edin-
    burgh University Press, 1996) 'The 1960s' pp. 120–48

Useful archive websites

**www.gla.ac.uk/services/specialcollections/collectionsa-z/
edwinmorganpapers/**
The Edwin Morgan Papers in the University of Glasgow
Library include many hundreds of original manuscript
poems and translations, essays and reviews on a wide range
of topics, thousands of letters to and from other poets,
papers related to his own publications and editorial work on
various journals, photographs taken on his travels, and his
mysterious Scrapbooks.

**www.scottishpoetrylibrary.org.uk/poetry/
edwin-morgan-archive**
This website from the Scottish Poetry Library features
pictures of all of the poet's publications, including rare and
out-of-print ones. There is biographical information, a time-
line of his work that includes comment from both the poet
and critics, live readings of various poems, and also ideas
for working with the poems individually or in groups.

www.edwinmorgan.com/
This website was designed in co-operation with the poet. It has pictures of many places in Glasgow and Scotland associated with his life and poetry, essays by European students on some of the *Sonnets from Scotland*, a bibliography, some poems, and links to other relevant websites. Some pages are still under construction.

www.glasgowlife.org.uk/libraries/the-mitchell-library/ special-collections/Pages/home.aspx
The Mitchell Library in Glasgow holds Edwin Morgan's Working Library in its Department of Special Collections. There are over 13,000 of the poet's books, many with his annotations.

9. INDEX OF TITLES

A single asterisk* indicates poems read by the poet on the ASLS CD *17 Poems of Edwin Morgan*, and a double asterisk** poems read on the ASLS CD *23 Poems of Edwin Morgan*.

17 POEMS OF EDWIN MORGAN
A Commentary

by Roderick Watson, with readings
by Edwin Morgan – volume 1

Audio CD   *£9.95*
ISBN 978-0-948877-62-9

Each poem here is read by
Edwin Morgan himself, followed
by informed and accessible
commentary by Professor Roderick
Watson of the University of Stirling.

This CD is an excellent tool for classroom study, as well as giving users a
chance to hear some of Scotland's best-loved poems read by the author
himself.

CONTENTS
Glasgow
1. To Joan Eardley
2. In the Snack Bar
3. Trio
4. For Bonfires

Instamatic Poems
5. Glasgow, 5th March 1971
6. Bangaon, India, July 1971
7. Leatherhead, Surrey, September 1971
8. One Cigarette
9. Strawberries

Saturn
10. Hyena
11. The Mummy
12. The Archaeopteryx's Song
13. From the Domain of Arnheim
14. The Computer's First Christmas Card
15. Message Clear
16. The Loch Ness Monster's Song
17. In Sobieski's Shield

23 POEMS OF EDWIN MORGAN
A Commentary

by Roderick Watson, with readings
by Edwin Morgan – volume 2

Audio CD £9.95
ISBN 978-0-948877-68-1

This CD brings together poems
from Morgan's most productive
phase of his middle period as a
poet, as well as a seletion of gems
from the final years of his life. The
readings are by Edwin Morgan himself and the critical commentary is by
Professor Roderick Watson of the University of Stirling.

CONTENTS

SCOTNOTES

Study guides to major Scottish writers and literary texts

Produced by the Education Committee
of the Association for Scottish Literary Studies